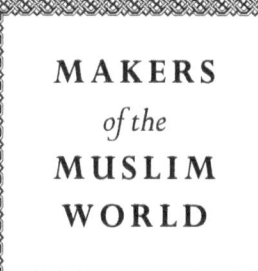

# Muhammad Abduh

# SELECTION OF TITLES IN THE MAKERS OF THE MUSLIM WORLD SERIES

Series editor: Patricia Crone,
Institute for Advanced Study, Princeton

*Abd al-Ghani al-Nabulusi*, Samer Akkach
*'Abd al-Malik*, Chase F. Robinson
*Abd al-Rahman III*, Maribel Fierro
*Abu Nuwas*, Philip Kennedy
*Ahmad al-Mansur*, Mercedes García-Arenal
*Ahmad ibn Hanbal*, Christopher Melchert
*Ahmad Riza Khan Barelwi*, Usha Sanyal
*Akbar*, André Wink
*Al-Ma'mun*, Michael Cooperson
*Al-Mutanabbi*, Margaret Larkin
*Amir Khusraw*, Sunil Sharma
*Ashraf 'Ali Thanawi*, Muhammad Qasim Zaman
*Chinggis Khan*, Michal Biran
*El Hajj Beshir Agha*, Jane Hathaway
*Fazlallah Astarabadi and the Hurufis*, Shazad Bashir
*Ghazali*, Eric Ormsby
*Husain Ahmad Madani*, Barbara Metcalf
*Ibn 'Arabi*, William C. Chittick
*Ibn Fudi*, Ahmad Dallal
*Ikhwan al-Safa*, Godefroid de Callatay
*Karim Khan Zand*, John R. Perry
*Mehmed Ali*, Khaled Fahmy
*Mu'awiya ibn abi Sufyan*, R. Stephen Humphreys
*Nasser*, Joel Gordon
*Sa'di*, Homa Katouzian
*Shaykh Mufid*, Tamima Bayhom-Daou
*Usama ibn Munqidh*, Paul M. Cobb

For current information and details of other books in the series, please visit www.oneworld-publications.com

MAKERS
*of the*
MUSLIM
WORLD

# Muhammad Abduh

MARK SEDGWICK

MUHAMMAD ABDUH

A Oneworld Book
First published by Oneworld Publications, 2010
Reprinted, 2020

© Mark Sedgwick, 2010

All rights reserved
Copyright under Berne Convention
A CIP record for this title is available
from the British Library

ISBN 978-1-85168-432-8
eISBN 978-1-78074-213-7

Typeset by Jayvee, Trivandrum, India
Cover and text designed by Design Deluxe
Printed and Bound in Great Britain
by Clays Ltd, Elcograf S.p.A.

Oneworld Publications
10 Bloomsbury Street
London, WC1B 3SR
England

Stay up to date with the latest books,
special offers, and exclusive content from
Oneworld with our newsletter

Sign up on our website
oneworld-publications.com

For Zahra

# CONTENTS

*Preface* xi

## 1 THE STUDENT 1
Tanta 2
Cairo 6
Afghani 8
Graduation 12

## 2 INTRODUCTION TO POLITICS 15
Muhammad Abduh's Teaching 16
Politics 18
Freemasonry 19
The Opposition Press 21
Intervention 24
Defeat 26

## 3 URABI AND EXILE 29
Muhammad Abduh the Editor 29
Muhammad Abduh and Urabi 31
Triumph and Renewed Defeat 33
Exile 35
Afghani, Muhammad Abduh and Islam 36
To Paris 42

## 4 PARIS 43
Muhammad Abduh and Wilfrid Blunt 45
*Al-Urwa al-wuthqa* 49

## 5  BEIRUT  57
The Break with Afghani  57
In Search of an Occupation  59
*Risalat al-Tawhid*  63

## 6  THE RETURN TO EGYPT  71
The National Courts  72
The Azhar Council  74
Appointment as Mufti  77
Law Reform  79

## 7  THE MUFTI  83
The Azhar Lectures  85
Newspapers  87
Education  91

## 8  THE FATWAS  95
Financial Fatwas  95
The Transvaal Fatwa  97
Muhammad Abduh's Methodology  99
Muhammad Abduh's Intentions  101

## 9  ADVERSITY  103
Opposition in the Press  105
Deteriorating Relations with the Khedive  107
Reactions to the Transvaal Fatwa  110
Resignation  111
Death  113
The Enemy of God?  113

**10 THE AFTERMATH** 115
    Public Life 115
    Islam 117
    Views on Muhammad Abduh 121
    Conclusion 126

*Glossary* 129
*Further Reading* 133
*Bibliography* 139
*Index* 145

# PREFACE

Muhammad Abduh (1849–1905), Mufti of the Egyptian Realm, is one of the most famous figures in recent Islam. In Egypt, he is now generally remembered as a great scholar and a patriot, a great renewer of Islam, one of those who awakened the nation – though the details of this greatness have grown somewhat fuzzy with time. Among scholars, in the Muslim world and the West, he is known as Islam's leading modernist. For some, his modernism consisted in creating a synthesis of Islam and modern thought; for others, it consisted in the bridge he built between the old world and the new. Some see him as having revived true Islam, and some see him as having proposed an alternative to true Islam. One question that this book attempts to answer, then, is quite what his modernism consisted in. Another question is where his modernism came from, and a final question is what happened to it after his death.

Muhammad Abduh was born into an Egypt that was an autonomous province of the ancient Ottoman Empire. He participated in a failed attempt at revolution, and died in an Egypt under British occupation. Politically, he lived through extraordinarily eventful times, and politics occupied him throughout his life, often more than Islam. Muhammad Abduh was, as a result of his initial education, a religious figure – a member of the ulema. He acquired this status almost by default, since at the time of his birth formal education in Egypt was almost exclusively religious. His appointment as Mufti made him one of the most senior three or four religious figures in the Muslim world, but his earlier career might equally have led to him becoming a government minister, a newspaper editor, or a university president – or a political prisoner, given that he was never afraid of risk and confrontation, and lived in a world where both were often dangerous. He did, in fact, spend some time editing a newspaper, and some time in prison.

Muhammad Abduh was one of the first Arabic-speaking Muslims to experience the West at first hand. Although he grew up in a purely Egyptian environment, he spent time in France and other European countries, learned French, and read deeply in nineteenth-century European social and political thought. Although he always remained Egyptian rather than European, he knew European ways well enough for his relationship with the very imperial British representative in Egypt, Lord Cromer, to become a real friendship. Although he remained a believing Muslim, he also took his Freemasonry very seriously. He certainly bridged two very different worlds, and tried to show others how this might be done. One part of his modernism, then, was to prefer a marriage of civilizations to a clash of civilizations.

Given this, it is strange that Muhammad Abduh's successor is commonly seen as Rashid Rida, that Rashid Rida's successor is commonly seen as Hasan al-Banna, the creator of the Muslim Brotherhood, and that the Muslim Brotherhood is seen as the distant origin of al-Qaeda. This is one of the paradoxes that this book explores.

This book builds on the research that has been done on Muhammad Abduh by many other scholars over the years. Its main contribution, I hope, will be in presenting a coherent picture of Muhammad Abduh. Many of those who have worked on Muhammad Abduh in recent years have done so from the perspective of some other issue that concerned them, and no full biography has been published by a Western scholar since 1933. As a result, it has sometimes been hard to judge various hypotheses against the big picture, which is what I have attempted to do while writing this book. When I have discarded a hypothesis as being too inconsistent with the big picture, I have generally not referred to it, given both limitations of space and the policy of this series, which calls for clarity. The specialist will, I hope, recognize which hypotheses I have discarded, and be able to read between the lines to see why.

In common with other volumes in this series, this book has no source notes. Suggestions for further reading, however, will be found at the end of the book, as will a bibliography giving my main sources. For those who are interested, further information on sources is available online at www.abduh.info. This website will also carry corrections of errors in the pages that follow (there will inevitably be some errors, for which I apologize in advance), such additional material as becomes available, a few images, and additional suggestions for further reading. Use of technical Arabic terms has been kept to an absolute minimum, but even so some have had to be used, and these are listed in a glossary.

I would like to thank the many students at the American University in Cairo (AUC) who took with me classes and seminars in which Muhammad Abduh was discussed, for the questions, objections, and suggestions that helped me refine my own understanding of Muhammad Abduh, and Dina Hamdy, who helped me research later views of Muhammad Abduh in Egypt. The 1933 biography of Muhammad Abduh was written by a scholar working at AUC, so it is appropriate that most of this book was written while I was also working at AUC. I would also like to thank two scholars who I have never met, but whose work was of great use: Mohamed Haddad and Indira Falk Gesink, who generously allowed me to make use of her unpublished PhD thesis. My thanks are likewise due to Patricia Crone, for her comments some years ago on the paper in which I first approached some of the issues that underlie this book, as well as for suggesting that I write it. Finally, I would like to thank two scholars who I know well, Elisabeth Sartain and Jakob Skovgaard-Petersen, for many fruitful discussions, and also for their comments on the manuscript of this book. In some cases, of course, disagreements remain.

Mark Sedgwick<br>
Aarhus University, Denmark<br>
February 9, 2009

# THE STUDENT

Muhammad Abduh was born to a small farmer in an Egyptian village in about 1849, the year of the death of Mehmet Ali, the Albanian soldier who had appointed himself governor of the Ottoman province of Egypt, rebelled against the Ottoman Empire, and successfully established himself as a powerful and independent ruler – at great cost to the small farmers of Egypt, upon whose forced labor he had built his power.

Mehmet Ali's strong rule did bring some benefits to small farmers such as Abduh ibn Hasan Khayrallah, Muhammad Abduh's father, since it ended the general disorder and periodic violence that had previously been the norm in the Egyptian countryside. Mehmet Ali's government also made improvements to rural irrigation systems, and promoted the growing of cotton, a crop for which Egypt became famous. The structure of the cotton trade, however, was such that most of the riches it produced went either to the Egyptian state or to merchants, and only rarely to the farmers who grew it. These farmers also had to provide forced labor for Mehmet Ali's various improvement projects, and conscripts for his armies. By 1840, according to some estimates, twelve percent of the working population of Egypt had been conscripted. Conscription was so unpopular that it was common for peasants to flee their villages or to maim themselves in order to avoid it. Muhammad Abduh's father was one of those who had fled his village, and the exact place of Muhammad Abduh's birth is thus unknown.

The Egyptian countryside became quieter after the death of

Mehmet Ali, and Muhammad Abduh grew up in the village of Mahallat Nasr, one of many small villages scattered around the green and fertile Delta area that stretches south from the Mediterranean coast to Cairo, watered by several branches of the Nile, one of which – the Rosetta branch – lay some eight miles to the east of Mahallat Nasr. In the other direction, also about eight miles away, lay the provincial capital, the town of Damanhur.

Though not rich, Muhammad Abduh's father was a substantial man in Mahallat Nasr, able to afford to marry a second wife. He was also wealthy enough to hire a private Quran teacher for his son. The only education then known in the Egyptian countryside started with the memorization of the Quran, a task that Muhammad Abduh had completed by the age of twelve. This was a later age than many, but equipped Muhammad Abduh to move on to the next stage, at the great mosque school in the town of Tanta, thirty miles from Mahallat Nasr. Muhammad Abduh's mother came originally from Tanta, and a relative taught at the school there, so there may have been some tradition of learning in his mother's family.

## TANTA

Muhammad Abduh arrived at Tanta in 1862, at the age of thirteen, shortly after Tanta had been connected to Cairo and Alexandria by a newly built railway. Tanta had been famous since the thirteenth century for its mosque, built around the tomb of Egypt's most revered Sufi saint, Ahmad al-Badawi, and during the mid-nineteenth century Tanta grew fast, becoming an important center for the cotton trade. As a result, a few European-style schools were just beginning to be established there by some of the newcomers whom the cotton boom was attracting – but these newcomers were Greek Christians, whose schools were not attended by Muslims. Muslims still had only one choice: the ancient school in the mosque of Ahmad al-Badawi.

Muhammad Abduh joined about one thousand other students there. Under the terms of the charitable endowment that had financed the Tanta school since the eighteenth century, education was free, and students also received basic food rations. Following immemorial practice, students gathered in circles around teachers, each of whom taught a particular text. Each text had to be learned by heart, and the teacher checked this. Students did not generally ask questions of the teacher, either during or after the session. One central discipline was the study of the meaning of the Quran, section by section, using such tools as grammatical and etymological analysis, reference to collections of *hadith* reports of the words and actions of the Prophet, and a complex methodology of *usul* or jurisprudence.

This was a system of education that Muhammad Abduh was later to criticize in the harshest terms, a system that has now generally been abolished, though it still survives in some places. It was not quite as bad a system as Muhammad Abduh later made out, however. It survived long enough in Morocco for a contemporary European researcher to be able to interview old men who had started their education in this way. The researcher concluded that the way the system actually worked was that the discussion that was essential for actually understanding the texts being studied took place informally. Students discussed texts with each other privately, and sometimes also discussed them with relations who were established members of the ulema, if they were fortunate enough to have such relations. Students who came from families in which scholarship was a tradition, then, had a definite advantage over outsiders. We know that Muhammad Abduh had a relation among the ulema of Tanta, but only a teacher of Quran recitation – the least prestigious branch of Islamic scholarship.

Whether or not Muhammad Abduh discussed the texts he was learning with a relation, he was not happy, and afterwards wrote that he had learned nothing during this period of his life. "The teachers were accustomed to use technical terms of grammar or jurisprudence which we did not understand," he later complained, "nor did they take any pauses to explain their meaning." After a year and a half, Muhammad Abduh ran away from Tanta to stay with some uncles, but was taken back by a stepbrother. He ran away again and returned to

Mahallat Nasr, determined to become a small farmer like his father. He got married, being by then sixteen, the normal age of marriage for a man who could afford to set up a household. We know nothing of his wife, who would probably have been younger, possibly as young as twelve. His father presumably approved of the marriage, which otherwise could hardly have taken place, and perhaps hoped that marriage would encourage Muhammad Abduh to settle down. After a forty-day honeymoon, Muhammad Abduh was again returned to the school in Tanta.

On his way back to Tanta, Muhammad Abduh stopped to stay with an uncle named Darwish, a Sufi. Sufism was widespread in rural Egypt, where in most cases it was a form of popular religion, associated with seasonal celebrations at the tombs of local saints, and with weekly meetings at which local men sat together and chanted the litany of one or another of the many different Sufi orders. Muhammad Abduh's uncle, however, was a different sort of Sufi, a follower of Muhammad al-Madani, one of the great shaykhs or spiritual masters in a movement of religious revival and reform that had started in the eighteenth century and lasted through the whole of the nineteenth century. Muhammad al-Madani was born in Medina, studied under the great shaykh Abu Ahmad al-Arabi al-Darqawi in Morocco, returned to Medina, and finally settled in Misrata, in what is today western Libya, where he established his own Sufi order, the Madaniyya. Under al-Madani's son, his following spread from Libya, Algeria, and Tunis to Egypt. Muhammad Abduh's uncle was a devoted follower of the Madaniyya, and had at one point made the arduous journey to Misrata to visit his shaykh.

The revivalist and reformist movement of which the Madaniyya was part was an international movement rather than a local one. It was also a scholarly and intellectual movement, not a form of popular religion, of which it was sometimes very critical. It stressed both spiritual experience and the proper practice of Islam, and was in contact with leading scholars in Medina who argued for closer adherence to the founding teachings of Islam and against *taqlid*, strict adherence to precedent. This combination of emphases – on the internal and on the external – was probably the main reason for its great success, along with the evident quality and charismatic nature of many of the chief figures associated with it, including al-Madani.

Muhammad Abduh's uncle pressed on him a book of the collected letters of al-Madani. After some days, Muhammad Abduh began to practice the litany of the Madaniyya, and after a few days more he found himself

> soaring in spirit in a different world from that which I had known. The way which seemed to me straitened, had widened out before me. The life of this world which had appeared great to me, had become small, and the acquisition of wisdom and the yearning of the soul towards God which had been small in my eyes had become great.

This is a description of exactly what following a Sufi practice such as that of the Madaniyya is meant to achieve – direct access to God, the feeling which Freud described as "the oceanic," though Freud did not explain it in terms of the divine. What is somewhat surprising is that it happened to Muhammad Abduh so quickly, but it evidently did happen, and the Muhammad Abduh who returned to the Tanta school was a changed man – not just married, but a Sufi.

Muhammad Abduh's experience and subsequent mystical orientation were not unusual. Many of his fellow students in Tanta were also Sufis, since at that time the ulema often combined the pursuit of external knowledge with the pursuit of illumination, the one found in schools such as Tanta and the other found at the hands of great shaykhs such as al-Madani. What is a little surprising is that Muhammad Abduh seems to have had no further contact with the Madaniyya. It is not known whether there were other Madanis in Tanta, but there were Madanis in Alexandria, and the journey to Alexandria would have been easy. Perhaps there was further contact, but Muhammad Abduh simply said nothing about it. Perhaps he was already inclined toward the independence that he would repeatedly demonstrate during the rest of his life.

## CAIRO

In 1866, at the age of about seventeen, Muhammad Abduh transferred from the Tanta school to the great school at the Azhar mosque in Cairo. This was a time-honored step, one necessary for those who wished to proceed to higher studies and so perhaps to a career in the ulema as a religious scholar, a preacher, or a judge. The Azhar was, like Tanta, free, and for centuries had been one of the four or five leading centers of scholarship in the Muslim world, and a well-trodden route by which men from villages like Muhammad Abduh's could rise to national prominence and honor.

It 1866, however, the Azhar was an institution in crisis. First, it was overcrowded – Azhar students were exempt from conscription, and so when conscription was introduced numbers of students had risen from the normal 2,000–3,000 to over 7,000. Numbers dropped after the end of Mehmet Ali's wars, but jumped again in 1866, and in 1867 there were almost 5,000 students. Second, the Azhar was in financial difficulties. Its senior scholars had assisted Mehmet Ali's rise to power in the first years of the century, but Mehmet Ali recognized that those who had helped him might one day help a rival, and so once he was firmly enough established he set about reducing the power of the ulema, and of the Azhar. He did this partly by encouraging splits and disputes in the Azhar's leadership, but most importantly by reducing the economic bases of the ulema's power – the "tax farms" or concessions that were the principal form of investment used by senior scholars, and the assets of the endowments that financed both them and the institutions they controlled. At precisely the point that the Azhar needed more money to pay stipends to more students and teachers, then, it found that it had less money. Despite this, the number of teachers increased, from around 30 at the beginning of the nineteenth century to 221 in 1867. This produced a respectable ratio of only twenty-one students per teacher, but it is likely that the quality of many of the new teachers was lower than that of the older teachers.

In addition to these problems, the behavior of students was often poor. Students are not the best behaved of adolescents, and overcrowding at the Azhar made things worse. In 1860, for example, only six years before Muhammad Abduh arrived, a dispute between students from Upper Egypt and students from Syria over sitting spaces for classes had developed into a brawl, and the Upper Egyptian students had blockaded the Syrian students in their dormitory. When soldiers were called to release the Syrian students, the Upper Egyptian students attacked the soldiers, and were only subdued by reinforcements. This riot was, perhaps unfairly, blamed on the rector of the Azhar, Ibrahim al-Bajuri, who was fired by the government and replaced by a four-man council. The Upper Egyptian students were much criticized – Ali Mubarak, a senior official in the Department of Education, alleged that they were in the habit of bringing their goats to class with them.

An attempt had been made to reform the Azhar the year before Muhammad Abduh arrived there, by Mustafa al-Arusi, a member of the Azhar Council who had been appointed rector of the Azhar by Egypt's new and ambitious ruler, Ismail. Al-Arusi introduced regulations which would have established central control of which teachers taught which texts in which locations, as well as obliging students to take exams. They would also have improved hygienic conditions in the dormitories. The resistance to these regulations from the Azhar's teachers was so great that when they petitioned Ismail for al-Arusi's dismissal, Ismail gave in. Muhammad Abduh, then, arrived at a famous but overcrowded institution where both teaching and hygienic conditions required improvement. The other students were often more interested in escaping conscription than in learning, were not subject to examination, and perhaps sometimes brought their goats to class. It was not until 1872 that a less ambitious reform succeeded in introducing a system of final examinations for a certificate known as the *alimiyya*, without which it was not allowed to teach.

According to his autobiography, Muhammad Abduh continued on the Sufi path as a student at the Azhar, though he makes no mention of any other Sufis, save for his uncle. Unlike most other Sufis,

Muhammad Abduh was evidently following an individual path, an approach discouraged among Sufis by the well-known saying: "He who has no shaykh has Satan for his shaykh." As well as continuing with the litany he had learned from his uncle, Muhammad Abduh followed a variety of ascetic practices – wearing a rough garment next to his skin, fasting frequently, staying up all night repeating various litanies. None of these practices were unusual among pious Muslims of a Sufi disposition, though Muhammad Abduh's practice of avoiding speaking to other people unless he had good reason to speak was slightly less common. After five years, in 1871, his uncle warned him that he was becoming too withdrawn, and advised him to increase his contact with others. This he did.

## AFGHANI

Up to this point, the story of Muhammad Abduh's life might be that of any of many thousands of other Egyptian Azhar students at any time during the previous several centuries. In 1872, however, when Muhammad Abduh was twenty-three, something very unusual happened. Muhammad Abduh joined a small group of students studying privately with a remarkable thirty-three-year-old Persian, Jamal al-Din al-Afghani. This was the first great turning point in his life.

There were then probably no other Persians at the Azhar, for the simple reason that Persia – the country now known as Iran – was Shi'i, following the smaller of the two rather different branches of Islam that had resulted from a split more than a thousand years before. Egypt, like most of the rest of the Arab world, followed the larger, Sunni, branch, and so the Azhar was also Sunni. Afghani, however, disguised his Shi'i origins by presenting himself as an Afghan, and so by implication a Sunni, since Afghanistan is mostly Sunni. Although a Persian would have had difficulty in passing as an Arab, it would have been easy for a Persian to pass as an Afghan, at least in the Arab world. In order to do so, however, a Persian would have had to adjust the details of his religious practice from the Shi'i to the Sunni norm, notably when praying. Observant Muslims – which would by definition include students at the Azhar – invariably pray the five daily ritual prayers, and when the time for a prayer comes, they often pray together. Sunni Muslims pray on prayer mats or carpets, which Shi'i Muslims only do with the aid of a *turba*, a small tablet of baked clay which they first place on the mat or carpet in front of them. Had Afghani used a *turba*, or had he prayed only on bare stone floors, his Shi'i identity would have become known immediately, since the *turba* is not used by Sunnis, and no Sunni would pray on a stone floor without a prayer mat. Since this did not happen, Afghani must have prayed without a *turba* – meaning that, in Shi'i terms, his prayers were neither valid nor acceptable. Afghani, then, had either converted from Shi'ism to Sunnism, or did not care about such details. According to his enemies, he was not a religious man – one account even has him drinking brandy and flirting with a European barmaid. This account is unconfirmed, and may have simply been an attempt to slander him.

Muhammad Abduh first met Afghani in 1869, during a stop Afghani made on his way from India to Istanbul, the Ottoman capital. In Istanbul, Afghani had established good relations with the director of the Institute of Arts (the Darülfünun), Taksin Pasha. The Ottoman title of pasha, rather like the English title of lord, indicated considerable wealth, a senior government position, or both. Taksin's Institute of Arts had just been established as part of the Ottoman Empire's great effort to modernize in order better to compete with the European empires that threatened it, an effort similar to the program that Mehmet Ali and Ismail were responsible for in Egypt. Afghani was also appointed to the Ottoman Council of Education. In 1871, however, outrage following Afghani's contribution to an evening lecture series at the Institute of Arts was the occasion for the closure of that institution, and led to Afghani's own expulsion from Istanbul – the immediate cause of his presence in Cairo. The lecture series was on the thoroughly nineteenth-century topic of "Progress in the Sciences and Industries," and in this context Afghani had apparently defined prophecy as a form of craft, and perhaps even suggested that philosophers were in some way superior to prophets. If true, this would inevitably have caused outrage. The text of Afghani's lecture does not survive, so it is not clear whether the objection was to what he actually said, to what he was thought to have said, or merely to the fact that the nature of prophecy was being discussed in a forum outside the control of the ulema. Whichever was the case, he left for Cairo.

In Cairo, Afghani attracted the patronage of Mustafa Riyad Pasha, who was in some ways the Egyptian equivalent of his former sponsor in Istanbul, Taksin Pasha. Riyad would play an important part in the lives of Afghani and Muhammad Abduh over the next few years, as well as in the history of Egypt. He was the Turkish-speaking son of an Ottoman official who had been director of the mint under Mehmet Ali, and was perhaps of Jewish origin. After a period in the army, he had held three provincial governorships before serving as treasurer under the Khedive Ismail – the title khedive had been chosen as a compromise between king and prince, and was held only by the hereditary ruler of Egypt in succession to Mehmet Ali. Riyad's career was interrupted by a clash with the khedive that led to his dismissal in 1868, but soon recovered. He was appointed director of education in 1873, and later became prime minister. Riyad evidently appreciated Afghani, since he awarded him a small stipend. Afghani took lodgings near the Azhar, and taught privately there and in a neighboring café, initially hoping to return to Istanbul.

As well as Muhammad Abduh, Afghani's regular students at this time included Saad Zaghlul, a younger Azhar student, Abdullah al-Nadim, who was about Muhammad Abduh's age, and another younger man, Adib Ishaq. All became friends, and all later went on to important positions – Nadim and Ishaq as prominent journalists, and Zaghlul as a great prime minister of Egypt after the First World War. Over the years, Muhammad Abduh would gradually part company with most of his associates from this period, but Zaghlul remained close to him for the rest of his life.

Afghani, whose earlier education in Persia had given him an excellent knowledge of Arabic, read with Muhammad Abduh and the others classic texts that were fairly standard in Persia, but far from standard in Cairo, notably works on philosophy in which there was then little interest in the Sunni world. These included, for example, the *Kitab al-isharat wa 'l-tanbihat* ("Book of directives and remarks") of Ibn Sina (Avicenna), who was best known in medieval Europe for his medical works, but who was also a philosopher in the tradition of Aristotle, Plotinus, and al-Farabi (Alfarabius). They also read together works that were not standard in Persia or in Cairo – Ibn Khaldun's *Muqaddima* ("Introduction"), which sets out a complex philosophy of history, and translations of European works.

Muhammad Abduh was as struck by Afghani's method of teaching as by his texts, for rather than teaching by rote as was done in Tanta and at the Azhar, Afghani actually discussed the texts he was teaching, encouraging, and asking his own when none were forthcoming. Even more, in Muhammad Abduh's own words, "he was not satisfied with an understanding of the book and assent to the opinions of the writer." Like some of the texts Afghani taught, such a method was standard in the schools of Persia. It was the beginning of the development of a critical and inquiring approach to knowledge for Muhammad Abduh, Zaghlul, and the others.

Two years after meeting Afghani, in 1874, Muhammad Abduh wrote his first book, *Risalat al-waridat fi sirr al-tajalliyyat* ("An essay on mystical inspirations from the secrets of revelation"). This is traditional in form but unusual in content, reflecting what he had learned from Afghani. It was not published in Muhammad Abduh's lifetime, but gives an excellent idea of what he had been studying. It starts with a discussion of philosophical proofs for the existence of God, based on Ibn Sina, and differing in some respects from the conception of the relations between God and creation then accepted at the Azhar. From this it moves on to a cosmology that shows the influence of the Shi'i philosopher Mulla Sadra and the School of Isfahan, and then to a discussion of prophecy that again follows Ibn Sina more than the Azhar. It is, in short, a work that owes as much or more to the Shi'i mystical philosophy that Afghani had learned, and was now evidently teaching, than to anything then visible in Cairo. It is also a continuation of the mystical approach to Islam that Muhammad Abduh had learned from his Sufi uncle, so the debt may not be to Afghani and Shi'ism alone: such works as Muhammad Abduh had read with Afghani had once been studied and appreciated in Cairo too, and although there is no evidence of much interest in them during the nineteenth century, there is equally no evidence that an interest in some of them had not survived, at least in restricted circles.

The *Risalat al-waridat* was followed in 1876 by a similar work, again unpublished in Muhammad Abduh's lifetime, *Al-taliqat ala sharh al-Dawani li'l-aqaid al-Adudiyya* ("A gloss to the commentary of al-Jalal al-Dawani on the *Dogmatics* of Adud al-Din al-Iji"). It has been argued, however, that the gloss is actually Afghani's, not Muhammad Abduh's.

Muhammad Abduh was twenty-three when he met Afghani, and through him encountered both the highly sophisticated Persian tradition of philosophy and works of modern European thought. As a result, his intellectual world became very different from that of his contemporaries at the Azhar. His earlier studies had prepared him for the encounter with Afghani, but provided little to satisfy his intellectual curiosity. Afghani's teaching, then, began to fill an almost blank page. At first, it was the Persian philosophy that had the greatest impact; later, it would be the European works. In later life, Muhammad Abduh did not adhere closely to the philosophical views he learned from Afghani, but he did continue to demonstrate the same intellectual independence as he showed in the *Risalat al-waridat*.

## GRADUATION

Predictably, Muhammad Abduh's new interests and views got him into difficulties at the Azhar, where rumors began to circulate to the effect that he was a Mutazilite – a member of a theological school that had ceased to exist some seven centuries before, although its doctrines were still known. These doctrines were objectionable to the Sunnis, but less so to the Shi'a, so Muhammad Abduh may well have expressed approval of one or more positions that were correctly identified as being of Mutazilite origin. Characteristically Mutazilite positions include views on the nature of God and on divine justice and free will that Sunni scholars rejected. Most important were the Mutazilite views on the relative authority of reason and revelation. For the Sunni scholars of the Azhar, the sole valid criterion of good and evil was that which God had revealed through the Prophet. For the Mutazilites, however, reason was also capable of deciding what was good and what was evil, though not in contradiction to revelation – a position which the Shi'a also hold. Given Muhammad Abduh's later enthusiasm for reason, this may have been the position which got him into trouble.

In general, however, Muhammad Abduh seems to have been somewhat circumspect. As a senior student, he taught some texts to other students, notably a fairly standard Sunni commentary by Saad al-Din al-Taftazani on the *Aqaid* ("Dogmatics") of Umar al-Nasafi. The text was not in itself problematic from the perspective of the Azhar, but it was not normally taught at the level that Muhammad Abduh taught it – and also presumably not normally taught by a student. Had Muhammad Abduh taught the views he had expressed in the *Risalat al-waridat*, he would have got into much more serious difficulties.

By his own later account, Muhammad Abduh denied following the Mutazila on the basis that if he had rejected strict adherence (*taqlid*) to one group, he would not take up strict adherence to another. On this basis, following the intervention of the rector of the Azhar on his behalf, he passed the final oral examination and, in 1877, received the degree of *alimiyya* which allowed him to teach. This story is slightly unlikely, however, for the simple reason that the necessity for *taqlid* was then generally accepted by all at the Azhar, and so a student who attempted to defend himself from one charge of heresy by proposing what was in effect an alternative heresy would hardly have improved his position. As will be seen, Muhammad Abduh later became a firm and public opponent of *taqlid*, and may even have first learned this from his Sufi uncle, but his later recollection of his response to charges of heresy may have exaggerated the extent of his defiance in 1877. He was probably less outspoken and more apologetic.

In 1877, then, Muhammad Abduh had entered the world of the Egyptian ulema as a qualified scholar at an institution that was still without rival in the Muslim world, despite its various problems. His horizons were far broader than those of the vast majority of his colleagues, and some of his more private views were closer to Shi'i than to Sunni Islam. He was also a member of a group of followers of an unusual émigré Persian, with connections to a rising politician, Riyad Pasha.

# INTRODUCTION TO POLITICS

After graduating with his *alimiyya* degree in 1877, at the age of twenty-eight, Muhammad Abduh was entitled to teach at the Azhar, which he did for two years until 1879, when he was banished from Cairo as a result of his political activities. Probably through the intervention of Jamal al-Din al-Afghani's patron Mustafa Riyad Pasha, he was also employed to teach at the rival Dar al-Ulum, a smaller institution that had been established five years earlier as a teacher training college on contemporary French lines, as part of a general reform of education that was one of the major projects of the new khedive, Ismail. Muhammad Abduh also held a third teaching post, at the Khedival School of Languages, where he taught Arabic. The duties attached to these teaching posts were evidently not excessive, since Muhammad Abduh still had time for journalism, and for participation in Afghani's political activities.

Muhammad Abduh continued to dress as an Azhari, wearing the turban of a religious shaykh rather than the fez that was becoming the standard wear of the modern government official or intellectual, generally worn with European dress or with military uniform. His activities over the years following his graduation, however, had little or nothing to do with Islam. Although he would later became world famous as a religious figure, we catch only occasional glimpses of his own stance on religious questions during this period.

Though he did not himself play a leading role in either journalism or politics between 1877 and 1879, Muhammad Abduh was a member of a group that tried to take advantage of the deteriorating position of the khedive to replace khedival absolutism with constitutional representative government. He participated at close quarters in extraordinary events that must have had a deep impact on a man in his late twenties, and shifted his attention from mystical Islam and philosophy to politics.

## MUHAMMAD ABDUH'S TEACHING

The classes for which Muhammad Abduh is remembered were on philosophy, history, and what would now be called sociology and political science. At the Azhar, where teachers still selected their own texts, he taught the *Tahdhib al-akhlaq* ("Training in ethics") of Ahmad ibn Miskawayh, and a translation of the *History of Civilization in Europe* of François Guizot. These were both highly unusual works. Ibn Miskawayh was a remarkable historian and philosopher of the tenth century who drew deeply on the Greek tradition, notably on Aristotle's *Nicomachean Ethics*, as well as on Islam. Guizot was even more remarkable.

Now generally remembered only as a nineteenth-century French prime minister, Guizot was once extraordinarily famous as a historian, appointed professor of modern history at the Sorbonne at the age of twenty-five. His *History of Civilization in Europe* followed the basic model of historical development with which most non-specialist Westerners today are familiar, and with which historians today would in part disagree. According to this model, the rational light of the ancient world was lost at the start of the dark ages, replaced by "theocratic" government that extinguished reason. Then came the Reformation, which Guizot called "the insurrection of the human mind against absolute power in the intellectual order." Two further developments showed the way to the civilized ideal of liberal pluralism – the revolution against the absolutism of King Charles I in England that led ultimately to representative government, and the Enlightenment in France that led to the rediscovery of reason.

What Guizot added to this narrative was a focus on social and intellectual history, and on the complex relationship between them and political history. Such an approach is fairly standard nowadays, but was pioneering in 1828, when Guizot's book was first published. The bureaucratic centralization of eighteenth-century France, for example, was seen by Guizot as leading to a deterioration in the character of individual Frenchmen – the political influencing the social. The exposure of the crusaders to new ideas in the East was seen as leading to an opening of the European mind, and so to an increase in liberty and an improvement in the character of individual Europeans – the intellectual influencing the political and the social.

The *History of Civilization in Europe* was important for the development of the thought of Alexis de Tocqueville, of John Stuart Mill, and of Karl Marx. It was also important for the development of the thought of Muhammad Abduh, who accepted not only Guizot's historical narrative, but also many of his other views – the negative impact on the individual of absolutism and "theocratic" rule, for example, and the positive impact on society as a whole of individual reason. Guizot, who opposed the attempt of the Bourbon Restoration to re-establish a version of the social and political system that had existed in France before the French Revolution, had a political agenda when he wrote his *History of Civilization in Europe*. Both book and author took a very clear side in the culture wars that split France for most of the nineteenth century. Muhammad Abduh seems to have adopted a political agenda that was not much different from Guizot's, perhaps encouraged by echoes of Guizot in some of the classic Islamic texts he knew.

At the Dar al-Ulum, Muhammad Abduh taught Ibn Khaldun's *Muqaddima*, the work on the philosophy of history to which he had previously been introduced by Afghani. On the basis of these lectures, he wrote his third book, *Falsafat al-ijtima wa al-tarikh* ("The philosophy of society and history"), the manuscript of which was lost when he was banished in 1879. It probably applied Guizot's model to Arab history. Certainly, when Muhammad Abduh turned again to Arab history in about 1885, Guizot's influence is very visible in the *Risalat al-tawhid* ("Essay on theology").

## POLITICS

Mehmet Ali had been an absolute ruler, and Egyptian politics had since then been mostly court politics. An opportunity for others to intervene in the political process, however, was provided by the gradual erosion of the Khedive Ismail's power in the face of increasing European intervention after Egypt defaulted on her international debt in 1876. This default led to the creation of a Commission of the Public Debt, which included representatives of foreign banks, and to joint European and khedival control over the revenues raised by the Egyptian Railways and the Port of Alexandria. A Commission of Inquiry, established in April 1878, started by investigating the possibility of confiscating some of the khedival estates, and ended as almost a shadow government. As the khedive progressively lost control of Egypt's finances to the Commission, a number of leading politicians began to promote their own solutions to Egypt's financial problems, and also to promote their own visions for Egypt's political future, often in opposition to the khedive, and sometimes in cooperation with the French and British governments. One of the first major figures to go into opposition was Afghani's patron Mustafa Riyad Pasha, who had been appointed to the Commission of Inquiry by the khedive, but soon began to operate independently.

The exact nature of Afghani's relationship with Riyad during this period is not known. It seems that he moved from supporting Riyad to promoting his own agenda, carrying with him the group of followers that included Muhammad Abduh. Although Afghani had been involved in education in Istanbul and had been passing his time in Cairo teaching young men such as Muhammad Abduh, he was first and foremost interested in politics. Before moving to Istanbul, he had been a close adviser to Muhammad Azam Khan, prince of Kabul and ruler of much of Afghanistan, until the prince was displaced by his half-brother Shir Ali. After leaving Cairo, Afghani would again be involved in politics at a high level in Persia, and then finally would be carefully excluded from politics by the Ottoman sultan, who treated him with honor but placed him under house arrest. Afghani's ability to gain quick access to the highest political circles in several different countries is striking, and hard to explain. He was later described by a pupil of Muhammad Abduh as "a revolutionary whose patriotic spirit descended from Garibaldi and whose hatred of existing institutions, and inclination towards radical means, descended from Bakunin," but neither Garibaldi nor Bakunin enjoyed Afghani's easy access to princes and crowned heads.

## FREEMASONRY

Afghani's entry into Egypt's political life came partly through his relationship with Riyad, who played a leading political role, and partly through his membership of a key Masonic lodge, the Kawkab al-Sharq ("Star of the East"), to which he had been introduced in 1875 by Raphael Borg, a Maltese who was serving as the British vice-consul in Cairo and who was the master of the District Grand Lodge. Afghani was already a member of an Italian Masonic lodge.

Freemasonry had become popular across Europe during the eighteenth century. It was in theory a voluntary and philanthropic brotherhood that stood above religion and politics. It was also secret, both with regard to details of the membership of individual lodges and with regard to the rituals and discussions that happened inside them. The rituals, which have become known in several versions, are elaborate. Their symbols relate on the one hand to the craft of the stone mason and architect, and on the other to moral and ethical qualities. They are both a means of instruction and a focus for reflection. While in one sense these rituals are definitely religious, they are not specific to any religion. Except in Scandinavia, Freemasons are not required to be Christians.

Discussions in Masonic lodges take two forms: formal discussions in a set place during a long ritual, and informal discussions among members of a lodge after a ritual has been completed, often over dinner. For Masonic purposes, it is the formal discussions that matter; for general purposes, the informal discussions may matter more.

Sometimes they are purely social, but sometimes they are the occasion for making arrangements of various sorts between men who may be rich or powerful, and who know they can trust each other. Many of Afghani's fellow members of the Kawkab al-Sharq were both rich and powerful.

Freemasonry is nowadays considered by most Muslims to be something definitely un-Islamic that no Muslim should be involved in, but this view was not held among the Muslim elites of Egypt and the Ottoman Empire during the nineteenth century. Views on the compatibility of Freemasonry and of Christianity have also varied from time to time and place to place. Freemasonry had first become established in Egypt during the reign of Mehmet Ali with the foundation of several lodges answering to the Grand Orient in Paris, led briefly by Prince Muhammad Abd al-Halim, a son of Mehmet Ali who hoped to succeed Ismail as khedive until Ismail changed the rules of succession in favor of his son Tawfiq. Banished in 1868, Prince Abd al-Halim became a persistent opponent of both Ismail and, later, Tawfiq.

Afghani's lodge, Kawkab al-Sharq, had been established under the United Grand Lodge of England in 1871, joining eight other "English" lodges and the earlier "French" lodges. It was unusual in that it carried out its proceedings in Arabic rather than a European language. Its members included the khedive's son and heir Prince Tawfiq, leading politicians such as Muhammad Sharif Pasha, a graduate of the French St. Cyr military academy who had served as a minister in several Egyptian governments, and grandees such as Butrus Ghali Pasha (a descendant of whom later became secretary general of the United Nations) and Sulayman Abaza Pasha (whose descendants remain rich and influential in Egypt even today). Several of Afghani's circle joined this lodge with him, including Muhammad Abduh and Saad Zaghlul. As a result, Muhammad Abduh – in his late twenties, the son of a small farmer from a village in the Delta – found himself in close contact with the highest of Egypt's elite. Such social mixing is not unusual in Masonic lodges, since it is a key principle of Freemasonry that all Masons are equal brothers within the lodge, irrespective of differences of class or religion.

The enthusiastic participation of Egyptians such as Muhammad Abduh in Freemasonry was later explained by Alexander Broadley, a British Freemason and the lawyer who defended Muhammad Abduh and others after the failure of the Urabi Revolt:

> The Egyptian patriots found a strange fascination in the mystic tie which was to unite all men in the common bond of liberty, and believed the same machinery which had helped the Italians in their struggle for freedom and unity would materially assist the Egyptian cause.

Broadley's explanation is probably the right one. Although the English lodges were often conservative and part of the establishment, others were not. Freemasonry is in theory non-political, but there is no ban on the promotion of general human welfare, an activity that can often take very political forms. Since Freemasons take their vows of secrecy very seriously, Masonic lodges lend themselves well to revolutionary activity – they are very hard for outsiders, including spies, to penetrate. As Broadley recalled, Freemasonry had been central to the efforts of the Italian revolutionaries during the Risorgimento. It would later play a similar role for the Turkish revolutionaries of the Committee of Union and Progress who took power in the Ottoman Empire in 1908. In the end, it never played quite such a role in Egypt, but through the members of the Kawkab al-Sharq, it came close to such a role. Afghani, then, was trying to use Freemasonry in a way that it had already been successfully used before, and would be successfully used again.

## THE OPPOSITION PRESS

The most visible activity of Afghani's group was in the field of journalism, then in its infancy in Egypt. Afghani encouraged Yaqub Sannua, a playwright who had once been welcomed as "Egypt's Molière" by the khedive, to start a satirical political newspaper, *Abu naddara al-zarqa* ("Mr Sunglasses" – a reference to Sannua's own nickname). This was only the fourth private newspaper in Egypt's history, and only one of the other three, *Al-Ahram* ("The pyramids," established in 1875), had survived for more than a few issues. *Abu naddara* was the first newspaper ever to use the colloquial Arabic spoken by normal Egyptians rather than the less-accessible formal language of scholarship. It was also the first Egyptian newspaper to publish cartoons, and was remarkable for its biting satire. Although it only survived for fifteen issues before it too was closed down, it invented Egyptian popular journalism.

*Abu naddara* was extraordinarily popular, which was one of the reasons Ismail banned it and sent Sannua into exile. It was replaced almost immediately, however, by *Misr* ("Egypt"). *Misr* was started by Adib Ishaq, a Freemason who had studied under Afghani with Muhammad Abduh, using a permit to publish obtained with the help of Riyad. *Misr* was thus more tightly connected to Afghani and Riyad than *Abu naddara* had been. It became the leading opposition newspaper, probably surviving because the increasing weakness of Ismail's position made it impossible for him to close it.

*Misr* was joined by several other papers, all of which were edited by followers of Afghani: *Al-Tijara* ("Commerce"), also edited by Ishaq, in 1878, *Mirat al-sharq* ("Eastern mirror") in 1879, edited first by Salim Anhuri and then by Ibrahim al-Laqqani, and *Misr al-fatat* ("Young Egypt"), again edited by Ishaq. By 1879, then, almost the whole of the Egyptian press – other than *Al-Ahram* and the official government papers – was edited by followers of Afghani, with contributions by others in the group. Muhammad Abduh, for example, wrote in *Al-Tijara* and *Mirat al-sharq*, as did Abdallah al-Nadim and Salim al-Naqqash, who coined the famous slogan "Misr li'l-Misriyyin" ("Egypt for the Egyptians"), which was still in use seventy years later, and remains well known today.

All these newspapers took much the same line: on behalf of the oppressed ordinary citizen, they attacked the khedive and the foreign bankers and governments who were increasingly taking control of Egypt's affairs, especially the British government. They argued for an Egyptian renaissance against both despotism and foreign rule. They were remarkably radical for the period. Adib Ishaq wrote with approval of all enemies of "despotism and the tyranny of tradition" who attempted to "light the way for liberty." He approved not only of the French Revolution of 1789, but also of contemporary revolutionaries everywhere, including those who would today be called terrorists, and were then as generally condemned as terrorists are today, though different words were then used. He praised Prussian socialism and Russian Nihilism. He welcomed the shooting of a Russian chief of police in 1877 by the young female Nihilist Vera Zasulich, and attempts on the life of the German kaiser and the shah of Persia. The attempt on the life of the shah that he welcomed was made by Babis, members of a Persian religious movement that later gave rise to the Baha'is. The Babis were in violent conflict with the Persian state as a result of that state's attempts to suppress them, but even so were and are generally understood as a religious rather than a political movement. For Ishaq, however, they were a "manifestation of the fire of liberty in the East."

Afghani wrote mostly against the British, whose imperialism he had seen at first hand as a young man in India, and also wrote cautiously in favor of the Russians and French, who he evidently saw as a counterbalance to the British. He also stressed the need for unity across religions against the common European threat, referring approvingly to Hindu–Muslim unity in India during the Mutiny of 1857, and criticizing the way in which followers of different religions "split their community and incite division and animosities." Founders of religions, such as Zoroaster, Jesus, and Muhammad, in contrast called for "the recognition of the origin of truth – that is, God – and the call to virtue and the practice of good." This rather utilitarian view of religion was not unusual in Europe in the late nineteenth century, but was as unusual in Egypt as was Adib Ishaq's praise for Russian Nihilism.

Although this opposition press referred to religion – as in the article by Afghani just referred to, and as when *Al-Tijara* argued that "patriotism is a religious duty, and defense of the homeland is jihad" – it was in no way Islamic. Sannua was a Jew, and Abib Ishaq (whose newspaper called for jihad) and Salim al-Naqqash were both Syrian Christians. This Christian presence was partly because many Syrian Christians had moved to Egypt in search of opportunity, and partly because modern political doctrines were especially attractive to religious minorities in the Muslim world. The older Ottoman conception of the community, which was primarily religious, excluded them, while the newer European conception of the nation that ignored religion included them. Jihad fought on behalf of the homeland was obviously a more attractive idea to a Christian than jihad fought on behalf of Islam.

The national consciousness that the opposition press was calling for did not yet really exist. On the one hand, older religious conceptions of the community were very widespread. On the other, Egypt in the 1870s was a remarkably cosmopolitan place. The ruling elite still spoke Ottoman Turkish rather than Arabic, and employed foreign experts in senior positions without hesitation – the chief of the army's General Staff, for example, was General Charles Stone Pasha, an American who had defended Washington, DC during the Civil War. Afghani himself, of course, was neither Egyptian nor a Sunni Muslim.

## INTERVENTION

As opposition to Ismail increased during 1878, Afghani's group added more direct action to journalism. The group, initially one within Kawkab al-Sharq, took a more distinct organizational form. Afghani became president of Kawkab al-Sharq, but some Egyptian Freemasons objected that he was straying from the Masonic principle of standing above politics – as, indeed, he was. Afghani and his followers considered this objection the result of cowardice, though, not of adherence to Masonic principle. Afghani changed his lodge's obedience from the United Grand Lodge of England to the Grand Orient in Paris – the Grand Orient was less averse to political activity than the United Grand Lodge. This attempt to defeat opposition evidently failed, however, and Afghani's group left Kawkab al-Sharq to form a new "national" lodge, also under the Grand Orient. According to one source, membership of this new lodge, the name of which is not known, soon reached about 300. Its members were organized into different sections for different political purposes.

One member of the Kawkab al-Sharq who followed Afghani into the new "national" lodge was Major Latif Salim, director of the Military College. In February 1879, as the financial crisis continued, the government of Nubar Pasha, an ambitious politician who was attempting to form a constitutional government opposed to Ismail but on good terms with the British, was forced to place a large number of army officers on half pay. Coming on top of the failure to pay salaries that were previously due, this brought discontent in the army to a dangerous point. Major Latif Salim drew up a petition demanding payment of arrears of pay, and led some 400 or 500 officers to present the petition to the minister of war. On their way, however, Latif Salim's group met Prime Minister Nubar Pasha and the British-imposed minister of finance, Sir Rivers Wilson, apparently by accident. Both men were forced to take refuge in the Ministry of Finance. A riot developed, which was quelled only by the khedive himself, who promised the officers payment of their arrears.

As a result of this incident, the khedive dismissed the Nubar government. The European consuls, who had previously supported Nubar, were forced to accept that Nubar was unable to control a deteriorating situation. After some delay, a new government was formed under Prince Tawfiq, with Riyad as minister of the interior and minister of justice – a government close to the old Kawkab al-Sharq, then, installed following an incident that a member of Afghani's group had organized. Within a few weeks, this Riyad government was replaced by one led by Sharif Pasha. The Sharif government implemented a "national plan" for a purely Egyptian ministry answerable not to the khedive, but to a Consultative Chamber of Deputies. Followers of Afghani, notably Abd al-Salam al-Muwaylihi, a deputy and Freemason, played a leading part in pressing for this national plan. Correctly or not, the London *Times* identified al-Muwaylihi as a front for Afghani.

On the face of it, then, Egypt was becoming an independent constitutional monarchy, and Afghani's group was partly responsible for this – though the extent of Afghani's responsibility, and indeed what was really going on behind the scenes, is far from clear.

The Sharif government, however, was in fact composed mostly of men loyal to Ismail, and what at first appeared to be the triumph of constitutionalism and representative government quickly turned into the restoration of the khedive's autocracy. As the khedive's triumph became clear, Afghani tried various ways of saving the situation. He is said to have persuaded the prime minister to suggest to the khedive that he abdicate, a suggestion that was – not unsurprisingly – rejected. He visited the French consul in search of French support for the replacement of the khedive by Prince Tawfiq. He and Muhammad Abduh even discussed the possibility of assassinating the khedive, though their plans seem to have got no further than deciding that the Qasr al-Nil bridge would be a suitable place. It is not known which of the two first suggested the assassination, but it was probably Afghani rather than Muhammad Abduh, since Afghani was later implicated in the successful assassination of another monarch, the shah of Persia. Muhammad Abduh's part in the discussion suggests that he was an important member of the group, even though his name does not otherwise feature much.

The European powers were less concerned about renewed despotism than were Afghani and Muhammad Abduh, but they did object to Ismail's breach of international financial agreements. The Ottoman sultan was persuaded to depose Ismail, the khedive who had done more to bring Egypt into the modern world than anyone since Mehmet Ali. On June 26, Tawfiq became khedive in his father's place. A delegation of the Kawkab al-Sharq went to congratulate him.

## DEFEAT

Tawfiq, however, refused to accept the parts of the "national plan" that would have turned Egypt into a constitutional monarchy, and

Sharif Pasha resigned as prime minister. Afghani spoke publicly against Tawfiq in the important and central Hasan mosque, criticizing him as a tool of European interests. His speeches were fiery:

> You have been born into slavery and are living under despotism. For centuries, you have been under the yoke of conquerors and oppressors ... That which you earn by the sweat of your brow has been taken away from you without your knowledge ... Rise from your indifference! ... Shake off the dust of ignorance and indolence! Live free and happy like other nations – or else die as martyrs!

Some days after this speech, Afghani was arrested and put on a ship to India. Tawfiq informed the British consul that he had taken this step because Afghani had been "inciting the people to rebellion and ... attempting to propagate Nihilism." In a later letter to Riyad Pasha, Afghani said that he was told by different people that his expulsion was at the request of the ulema, of the European consuls, and of the khedive. He himself blamed his expulsion on the hostility of supporters of Prince Abd al-Halim, Tawfiq's predecessor as crown prince. All of this was probably true. Abd al-Halim would have been right to see Afghani as an enemy, as would Tawfiq. Afghani had also made enemies of the British by contact with the French consul and of the ulema by promoting ideas which were, if not exactly Nihilism, certainly highly objectionable to them. It was to be expected that the failure of his group's plans would lead to his arrest.

Other members of Afghani's group also suffered as Tawfiq attempted to re-establish khedival authority. *Misr al-fatat* was closed down, as was *Al-Tijara*. In September, Muhammad Abduh was arrested, and banished from Cairo to his native village, in internal exile. Muhammad Abduh's introduction to politics had seen the cause for which he was working briefly come close to success, but end in complete failure.

# URABI AND EXILE

Banished from Cairo after the failure of the attempt to transform Egypt into a constitutional monarchy, Muhammad Abduh spent some time in his village. He then moved from there to Alexandria, then to Tanta, and then to the outskirts of Cairo, where he stayed with an official on the board of education, Rifaa Bey. Muhammad Abduh evidently retained some of the contacts in political circles that he had made under Afghani's patronage. These contacts effected a reconciliation with Riyad Pasha, again prime minister, who pardoned him.

In September 1880, only one year after his banishment, Muhammad Abduh was appointed one of three editors of Egypt's official journal, *Al-Waqa'i al-misriyya* ("Egyptian proceedings"). He soon became the editor-in-chief, a position which also gave him official control of the rest of Egypt's press. This rapid reversal of fortunes reflected the ascendancy of Riyad, and probably also reflected a shortage of capable journalists.

## MUHAMMAD ABDUH THE EDITOR

*Al-Waqa'i al-misriyya*, which had been established in 1828 as an irregular four-page newsletter in Ottoman Turkish and (rather bad) Arabic, had by 1880 become a somewhat better bi-weekly newspaper in Arabic. Muhammad Abduh took steps to improve it further, persuading the prime minister to order government departments to submit to it regular accounts of projects proposed, in progress, and completed, and adding an editorial section. As overseer of the

Egyptian press, Muhammad Abduh also attempted to raise journalistic standards elsewhere, notably by calling for better Arabic. His requirement that reports critical of government officials be properly investigated before publication might be seen as an attempt to improve accuracy, or might be seen as an attempt to suppress reports critical of the prime minister and his colleagues.

Some of the editorials in *Al-Waqa'i al-misriyya* were written by Muhammad Abduh himself. Others were written by Saad Zaghlul and by Abd al-Karim Salman, whom Muhammad Abduh knew from the Azhar, and who had perhaps also been a member of the Afghani group.

Muhammad Abduh's editorials in *Al-Waqa'i al-misriyya* addressed social rather than political questions, expressing positions which have often since become generally accepted among Muslims, but were then novel and daring. The importance of education was a favorite theme, the topic of some fifteen percent of his articles. He warned against acquiring the trappings of European civilization without its substance, and against sending Muslim children to foreign, Christian schools. He called for the reform of character, especially among the peasantry, and condemned corruption and conspicuous consumption. He also attacked *bida*, a term which literally means 'innovation' in the sense of departure from the model of the Prophet Muhammad in religious matters, but which might also mean superstition. One particular target was the *dawsa*, a major annual festival during which the chief of a major Sufi order, the Saadiyya, rode on a horse over the bodies of a hundred or more of his followers, who lay face down on the ground for the purpose. Accounts differ as to whether or not injuries were frequent. Another target was polygamy, then a generally accepted form of marriage among Muslims. Muhammad Abduh advanced the ingenious argument, previously promoted in India by the modernist religious reformer Ahmad Khan, that although Islamic law permits polygamy in theory, it prohibits it in practice. A man is required to behave equally toward all his wives, which is in practice impossible. Hence a man is prohibited from marrying more than one wife.

Muhammad Abduh's editorials in *Al-Waqa'i al-misriyya* show, for the first time, his progressive social views, and also his views on education. He continued to hold these views for the rest of his life. The conviction of the importance of education in reforming Egypt was one that he shared with many others, including the former khedive Ismail. A well-educated population is still regarded today as necessary for development; its necessity was already clear in Egypt in the late nineteenth century, as a result of the severe shortage of men who could operate effectively in the new systems being copied from Europe.

## MUHAMMAD ABDUH AND URABI

The turbulent politics of Egypt in this period soon propelled Muhammad Abduh back from the social into the political arena. In February 1881, there was a repeat of February 1879's discontent among army officers, led this time by Colonel Ahmad Urabi, an officer who had no connection to the Afghani group. Urabi and his supporters intended to petition for the replacement of the minister of war by their own nominee, but were arrested before they could do so. A prearranged mutiny then freed them, and forced the installation of an Urabist candidate as minister of war.

At first, Muhammad Abduh continued to support the government, partly because he distrusted Urabi and his fellow officers, and partly because the Urabists were hostile to the Afghani group, for reasons that are not clear. In July, however, Riyad Pasha and the khedive attempted to reassert their control, causing the Urabists to form an alliance with the constitutionalists of 1879, and to launch a second mutiny in September, during which Urabists occupied the courtyard of the khedival palace. This resulted in the replacement of Riyad Pasha by Sharif Pasha as prime minister, and a renewed attempt to place khedival power under the control of a constitution. It also resulted in Muhammad Abduh's conversion to the Urabist cause. Disappointed when Tawfiq re-established autocracy after the fall of

Ismail, Muhammad Abduh saw another possibility of establishing "liberty" in Egypt, as he later wrote to Afghani.

As editor of *Al-Waqa'i al-misriyya* and chief censor, Muhammad Abduh was in a position to give real support to the Urabists and the constitutionalists, both by means of articles in *Al-Waqa'i al-misriyya* and by failing to exercise his powers as censor against Urabists such as Abdallah al-Nadim, who had formerly written in *Mirat al-sharq*, and who had now become known as *khatib al-thawra*, "the orator of the revolution." Press support for Urabi converted what was initially a military movement into something approximating a genuinely national movement for freedom from autocracy and from foreign control. The extent to which there was genuinely a national movement was hotly debated, both in Egypt and abroad, in the immediate aftermath of the movement's failure, and again in the 1950s after another Egyptian colonel – Gamal Abdul Nasser – seized power and gained popular support. There is evidence on both sides, but not enough to permit a decisive conclusion.

Muhammad Abduh developed constitutionalist political views in a number of articles. He called for a state based on law, which he interpreted not just as a constitutional system but as a system in which laws were relevant to the circumstances, and known to and understood by the people. The importance of the relevance and appropriateness of law was a conviction he would hold throughout his life. "Let it not be supposed," he wrote in *Al-Waqa'i al-misriyya* in December 1881, "that the just law based on liberty is that which is modeled entirely on the civil principles and political foundations of other countries ... Many a law is suited to the interests of one people but not to those of others."

On the whole, though, the example of Europe was beneficial. Egyptian society, Muhammad Abduh wrote, had been destroyed by rivalry to the point where each person had come "to restrict his attention to his own immediate concerns, and never to think of the rights of society." However, if people "learn something of the conduct of other nations they will recall that they once had rights as a group," and "as their social impulses grow in strength ... they will set to work to clear away the dross of their corrupted qualities." This was already happening, resulting in the calls for representative government which Muhammad Abduh himself was backing.

Although Muhammad Abduh's political positions were modern, they were modern by the standards of the nineteenth century, not those of today. He did not, for example, support democracy with a universal franchise – a system that was then found only rarely. It was proper, wrote Abduh, to exclude from the franchise "the lowest class of the workers, even if they are large in number, for they perform the function of deaf instruments, limited to bodily activity alone." This was a view that would have commanded general acceptance at the time in Britain and many other countries, though not in the United States.

It is at this point that we have the first physical description of Muhammad Abduh, from the pen of the Irish activist Wilfrid Blunt, who was in Egypt at the time. Blunt met and admired Muhammad Abduh, then "a man of about thirty-five, of middle height, dark, active in his gait, of quick intelligence revealed in singularly penetrating eyes, and with a manner frank and cordial and inspiring ready confidence." Another sketch is provided by Alexander Broadley, later Muhammad Abduh's defense lawyer:

> Perhaps the most gifted man in the ranks of the Egyptian Nationalists. An elegant writer, a profound Arabic scholar and an eloquent and impressive speaker, he exercised an appreciable influence among the more educated classes of his fellow-countrymen. He had unquestionably greatly helped to make public opinion a real factor in Egyptian progress.

## TRIUMPH AND RENEWED DEFEAT

In early 1882, with Urabi as minister of war and Prime Minister Mahmud Sami Pasha al-Barudi doing Urabi's bidding, the Urabists (if not exactly the constitutionalists) appeared to have triumphed. Urabi, however, had overplayed his hand. Britain and France, concerned that the Urabists threatened their financial and other interests, decided to support the khedive, and sent warships to Alexandria. By July the khedive had fled to European protection in Alexandria, where an outbreak of rioting finally triggered British military intervention. In September 1882, a British army defeated Urabi's forces at the battle of Tel al-Kabir and occupied Cairo. Urabi and his supporters, including Muhammad Abduh, were arrested. Muhammad Abduh was charged with "administering unlawful oaths" – apparently, an oath of loyalty to Urabi.

Alexander Broadley, the English lawyer sent by Urabi's British sympathizers to defend him, also took on the task of defending other imprisoned Urabists. When he visited Muhammad Abduh in jail, he found that

> his mind and body alike seemed crushed beyond hope of recovery by the cruel reaction born of shipwrecked hopes and the agony of despair. Like his fellows, he had been insulted and ill-treated in prison, but even his own account of his sufferings is weak and equivocal compared to theirs.

In general, Urabists with good connections to the elite escaped punishment. Urabi himself was tried, spared execution, and sent into permanent exile. Muhammad Abduh escaped trial as a result of Broadley's negotiations, but was sent into exile for three years. A year later he wrote to Afghani in harsh terms of the Urabists:

> These men donned the garb of prophets but followed the methods of tyrants; they spoke the words of learned men and were inwardly ignorant; they adopted our manner of calling for liberty, and were enabled by the power of the sword and the weakness of the government to convince the vulgar man that they stood for right and truth and the protection of the laws.

In the years since he graduated from the Azhar, Muhammad Abduh had twice been involved in attempts to reform Egyptian politics and society, and had twice been disappointed. On the first occasion, the cause of liberty had been defeated by the khedive, with British support. On the second occasion, the cause of liberty was defeated by the miscalculations of the Urabists, and by the British occupation of Egypt.

## EXILE

Exiled from Egypt in December 1882, Muhammad Abduh traveled to the Ottoman Empire, first to Damascus and then to Beirut. Little is known of how he spent his time in Damascus, save that he met the son of the Amir Abd al-Qadir, formerly leader of the armed resistance to the French occupation of Algeria, and briefly ruler of a small state recognized by France. After his defeat, Abd al-Qadir had spent some time in France as an honored prisoner, and had joined a Masonic lodge. After his release by Emperor Napoleon III, he moved to Damascus, where – as well as being awarded the Légion d'honneur for saving many Christians during a riot – he devoted the remainder of his life to the study of the works of the greatest of Sufi mystic philosophers, Muhyi al-Din ibn al-Arabi.

Abd al-Qadir became a central point in a group of religious reformers known as the Salafis (a group to which the well-known contemporary movement of the same name has no connection), and it has been suggested that through these contacts Muhammad Abduh met representatives of the Salafis. The name Salafi stressed the group's adherence to the doctrines and practices of the *salaf*, the first generations of Muslims after the Prophet, rather than to the later formulations of Islamic law that were then generally accepted. The Salafis rejected *taqlid* (strict adherence to precedent), as did Muhammad Abduh, but for somewhat different reasons. The Salafis were connected to the same earlier movement as the Madaniyya, the Sufi order to which Muhammad Abduh's uncle belonged, and wished to follow the earliest models of Islam more closely. This might have made Muhammad Abduh sympathetic toward them, but the later logic behind his rejection of *taqlid* was more utilitarian, as will be seen. Although he may have been in contact with these Salafis, then, it is unlikely that in the end he took much from them other than, perhaps, their reference to the *salaf*.

In 1883, Muhammad Abduh moved from Damascus to Beirut, a city which enjoyed relative autonomy under arrangements forced on the Ottomans by the European powers for the sake of the city's significant Christian population. In Beirut, he joined a small group of other Egyptian exiles, and was welcomed by local progressive intellectuals. He initially stayed with Muhyi al-Din Bey Humada, the reformist mayor of Beirut, before taking a house in the Zuqaq al-Blat quarter, the modern area of the city.

Among the exiles in Beirut were Ibrahim al-Laqqani, the former editor of *Mirat al-sharq* and a former member of the Afghani group in Cairo, and Abu Turab, Afghani's servant, who performed functions akin to those of Afghani's assistant. Al-Laqqani had arrived in Beirut with Abu Turab, whom he had met in a jail in Alexandria where the two were awaiting deportation. Abu Turab had accompanied Afghani to India, but had then returned to Cairo on a mission to recover Afghani's personal effects and money owed him by Riyad Pasha and Sharif Pasha. He had then been arrested. Al-Laqqani had presumably been arrested for participation in the Urabi Revolt.

## AFGHANI, MUHAMMAD ABDUH AND ISLAM

Contact with Afghani thus re-established, Muhammad Abduh wrote to his former teacher and leader, who had by then moved to Paris, requesting copies of his recent articles. Until this point there is evidence of the young Muhammad Abduh's views on political and social questions, but not on religious questions. As a result of Muhammad Abduh's renewed contact with Afghani, his views on religion become somewhat clearer, though not entirely clear.

Among the articles Muhammad Abduh received was one by Afghani that had been published in French in the *Journal des débats* on May 18, 1883 in response to a lecture by Ernest Renan, a renowned Orientalist. Renan's lecture, given at the Sorbonne, had been printed in full in the *Journal des débats* six weeks before, and had attracted much attention. Renan had argued, with some passion, that both Islam and the Arab spirit were hostile to science and philosophy, and that the famous Arab and Islamic scientists and philosophers of the past were in fact neither Arab nor Muslim. They were perhaps Arab by language, but were generally Persian in cultural and racial terms. Some were not Muslim, and those who were Muslim were "in internal revolt against their own religion."

Afghani replied that it was wrong to distinguish language from race in this way. "Human races can be distinguished only by language," he wrote, and no one seriously suggested that Mazarin and Bonaparte were Italian rather than French, despite their origins. Anyhow, the Arab spirit could hardly be thought hostile to science and philosophy given the speed with which it had advanced along "the path of scientific and intellectual progress," assimilating Greek and Persian science in less than a century. Afghani, however, accepted Renan's basic proposition concerning Islam – that it was hostile to science and philosophy. "It is evident that, wherever it became established, this religion sought to stifle science," he wrote. However, this was not the fault of Islam itself. "All religions are intolerant, each in its own way." Nor did this mean that Muslims could never develop science and philosophy. There was a general pattern whereby all peoples, at their origin, were necessarily governed by strict rules "imposed in the name of the Supreme Being, to whom their teachers attributed all events, without permitting them to discuss the advantages or disadvantages of this." This is how all peoples, Muslim, Christian or pagan, first emerged from barbarism. Christian societies had then moved forward from this first period "to advance rapidly on the path of progress and science." So might Muslim societies.

> I cannot but hope that Mohammedan society will one day break its bonds and walk resolutely on the path of civilization after the example of Western society for which the Christian faith, despite its rigors and its intolerance, has in no way been an insuperable obstacle.

In a letter in the next day's *Journal des débats*, Renan welcomed Afghani's article, and accepted that Muslim societies might indeed "arrive at that state of benevolent indifference [towards religion] in which religious beliefs become inoffensive," as had happened in many — but not all — Christian countries. "Reduced to the condition of individual and voluntary things, like literature or taste, religions change entirely," asserted Renan, an end that in the case of Islam could be best achieved by the spread of education.

When Afghani's article arrived and its full contents were explained to Muhammad Abduh by a translator, Muhammad Abduh decided that the article could not possibly be published in Arabic, which had been the original intention. Anything that seemed to hope for the decline of Islam would have been received very badly. Muhammad Abduh put the translator off with an excuse, and explained this to Afghani in a letter. He added:

> We regulate our conduct according to your sound rule: we cut off the head of religion only with the sword of religion. Therefore if you were to see us now, you would see ascetics and worshipers kneeling and genuflecting, never disobeying what God commands and doing all that they are ordered to do.

The exact meaning of this curious passage, contained in a letter that was not published until 1963, has been much debated, with much attention focusing on the possible meaning of the word "head" (*ras*). In his letter to the editor of the *Journal des débats*, Renan had described Afghani as "entirely free from the prejudices of Islam," adding that "his freedom of thought, his noble and loyal character, made me think whilst talking to him that I had before me, reincarnated, one of my old friends, Avicenna, Averroes, or another of those great infidels who for five centuries represented the tradition of the human spirit." Some have argued that Muhammad Abduh, like Afghani, was an infidel, "entirely free from the prejudices of Islam" in the sense of having left Islam. An alternative interpretation is that Muhammad Abduh and Afghani were simply free of the *prejudices* of Islam, an interpretation that seems more likely. In his article, Afghani was arguing that Muslim society would "walk resolutely on the path of civilization" when the habit of looking only to Islam and never to science or philosophy had been eliminated, not when Islam itself had been eliminated. That Renan hoped for a "state of benevolent indifference" did not mean that Afghani, or Muhammad Abduh, did. Whatever Muhammad Abduh meant by *ras*, he did not mean Islam as a whole.

Much has been read into a distinction between the masses and "a few select minds" made in the conclusion of Afghani's article:

> For so long as humanity exists, the struggle will not cease between dogma and free enquiry, between religion and philosophy, a desperate struggle in which, I fear, the victory will not be to free thought. The masses do not like reason, the teachings of which are understood only by a few select minds. Science, however fine it may be, cannot completely satisfy humanity's thirst for the ideal, or the desire to soar in dark and distant regions that philosophers and scholars can neither see nor explore.

Afghani, it has been suggested, was not himself religious, but recognized that religion was useful for the masses. This interpretation has been supported by one reading of a work of Afghani's that Muhammad Abduh did translate while in Beirut, *Haqiqat-i mazhab-i naichun* ("The truth about the naturist sect"), written in Persian, and published in Hyderabad in 1881. Abu Turab knew Persian, and worked with Muhammad Abduh on this translation, which was published in Arabic as *Al-radd ala al-dahriyyin* ("Refutation of the materialists") in Beirut in 1885. While Muhammad Abduh did not necessarily agree with every word written by Afghani in this work, it can safely be assumed that he did not disagree with its basic tenor.

Afghani's work was written during a controversy in India unleashed by the public endorsement of the laws of nature by Ahmad Khan, the Indian Muslim reformer whose ingenious argument that polygamy was forbidden in practice had been used by Muhammad Abduh in *Al-Waqa'i al-misriyya*. Ahmad Khan had addressed the relationship between nature and religion, a difficult issue for all religions during the late nineteenth century. The issue arose partly because of new scientific discoveries such as those of Darwin. Even before

Darwin, the discoveries made by early geologists had already undermined the previously accepted narrative of creation, common to Islam and Christianity. Darwin in a sense delivered the *coup de grâce* by arguing that the origin of species was not divine will but the consequences of random, chance events. A second problem was posed by what we would now call social science – rationalist and scientific analyses of human behavior that advanced explanations and prescriptions often at variance with religion. Ahmad Khan had grasped the bull by the horns, accepting the scientific understanding of nature, and proposing that "The work of God (nature and its fixed laws) is identical with the Word of God (the Quran)." This was not the only way in which he grasped a bull by its horns, however. A second issue that confronted Indian Muslims at the time was their relationship with the British rulers of India. Ahmad Khan advised absolute loyalty to the British crown, coupled with education along British lines. In 1878, he had founded a "Muhammadan Anglo-Oriental College" at Aligarh, modeled on the great British universities, and in 1878 he had accepted appointment by the British to India's Viceregal Legislative Council. In 1888, after these events, he was made a British knight.

Afghani took issue with Ahmad Khan, arguing against the "naturists" on two bases. First, he deployed philosophical arguments against the Darwinian view that chance could be a prime cause. Second, he argued for the social usefulness of religion, which the gross materialism of the naturists – among whom he included contemporary socialists – tended to destroy. Religion, he argued, is the only true basis for personal morality, social cohesion, and civilization in general.

One reading of this takes Afghani's emphasis on the social utility of religion together with his view that the masses want religion, and concludes that Afghani thought that religion was *only* for the masses, and that social utility was the only or main justification for it. An alternative reading notes that the fact that Afghani thought that religion had social utility did not mean that he thought that it had no other justification.

At the end of his book on the "naturists," Afghani argues that Islam is the best of all the religions, since it

> is the only religion that censures belief without proof and the following of conjectures; reproves blind submission; seeks to show proof of things to its followers; everywhere addresses itself to reason; considers all happiness the result of wisdom and clear-sightedness.

Afghani concludes:

> If someone says: If the Islamic world is as you say, then why are the Muslims in such a sad condition? I will answer: When they were [truly] Muslims, they were what they were and the world bears witness to their excellence. As for the present, I will content myself with this holy text: "Verily, God does not change the state of a people until they change themselves inwardly."

Afghani's characterization of Islam as "the only religion that censures belief without proof" requires comment. At the time, it was generally agreed among the Shi'a that Islam required an understanding of the logical proofs behind belief; this was not, however, the view of the Sunni ulema at that time. Afghani is writing, then, not of Sunni Islam as it then was, but of Islam as he – and presumably Muhammad Abduh – would have liked it to be: rational. If nature and Islam were one and the same for Ahmad Khan, reason and Islam were one and the same for Afghani and, as we will see, for Muhammad Abduh.

Read in this light, Afghani's response to Renan does not mean that science and philosophy may flourish in the Muslim world when Islam has passed, but that they may flourish when the opposition to reason that is associated with the current form of Islam has passed. Muhammad Abduh, then, seems to have agreed that the intolerance currently found in the Muslim world was a severe obstacle to progress, not that Islam itself was an obstacle to progress.

Although the precise religious stance of Afghani and Muhammad Abduh cannot be determined with certainty, then, it seems unlikely that they were the atheists that they have sometimes been made out to be. It is possible that they were liberal, but in some sense believing, Muslims.

## TO PARIS

Afghani evidently suggested to Muhammad Abduh that he join him in Paris, since Muhammad Abduh wrote to Afghani that he would certainly do this, were it not for his wife and children, who had accompanied him to Beirut. Muhammad Abduh later changed his mind, however, and did go to Paris. A curious exchange of letters between him and Prince Abd al-Halim survives, in which Muhammad Abduh writes that he and an unidentified Shubashi had arrived in Paris as Prince Abd al-Halim wished, and looked forward to receiving £100. Prince Abd al-Halim replied that he had never asked them to go to Paris, had only given Shubashi money in the past because Shubashi insisted, and was not going to work with them or with Afghani. Someone had evidently misled Muhammad Abduh, who had been introduced to one of the characteristics of the life of the political exile: the constant search for money from all available sources.

# PARIS

Muhammad Abduh arrived in Paris in 1884, joining Afghani and a number of other exiled Egyptians and Ottomans there. Paris was a natural destination for these exiles, as a place of relative safety and freedom, as the period's chief global center of culture and art, and as a city where French – then the most widely known international language – was spoken. Within thirty years, these Middle Eastern exiles would be replaced in Paris by refugees from the Russian revolution. It was only after the Second World War that the pre-eminence of French and Paris was challenged by English and America.

The Ottomans formed the largest group of exiles in Paris, engaging in often bitter émigré politics, publishing numerous émigré newspapers, and frequently spying on each other. The Ottoman government devoted such resources to paying spies and bribing journalists that one historian has speculated that the major source of finance for all these émigré activities was provided unwittingly by the Ottoman government.

The Egyptian émigré community was rather smaller. One of its earliest members was Afghani's friend Yaqub Sannua, who had moved to Paris after his satirical newspaper *Abu Nadara* had been closed by the khedive Ismail in 1877. Afghani had remained in contact with Sannua during the period he spent in India after his own expulsion from Egypt. Also in Paris were Ibrahim al-Muwaylihi, the brother of the Freemason and deputy who had supported the "national plan" under the khedive Ismail, and Ibrahim al-Laqqani, the former editor of *Miraat al-sharq* who had met Afghani's servant Abu Turab in an Alexandria jail and had been the means by which Muhammad Abduh re-established contact with Afghani. Adib Ishaq, formerly editor of *Misr*, was also in Paris, but seems to have held somewhat aloof from the others. His émigré newspaper supported Sharif Pasha, not Riyad Pasha, the former patron of the Afghani group.

In Paris, Afghani again became a focus for these men, as he had been previously in Cairo. Freemasonry seems not to have played a significant role on this occasion, although Afghani did apply for membership of a lodge in Paris. In Cairo it was necessary to organize clandestinely, but in Paris it was possible to organize openly, so long as the French government was not attacked. Afghani organized a group he called Al-urwa al-wuthqa, "The firmest bond," a phrase used twice in the Quran to indicate the value of faith in God: "Whoever submits himself wholly to God and is a doer of good, has indeed taken hold of the firmest bond" (Q. 31:22). Afghani, however, used the term metaphorically – his group focused not on submission to God but on politics.

Afghani's Paris group probably consisted of only a few people. He may have hoped that it would become as significant as some of the larger Ottoman émigré organizations, or as the group he had headed in Cairo, but this did not happen. The group may have been responsible for an attempt at intimidating some British officials in Egypt by sending threatening letters – the British authorities thought these probably came from Afghani – but its main activity was to publish a newspaper, also called *Al-Urwa al-wuthqa*, between March and October 1884. This newspaper was small (only four pages an issue), short lived (it published only eighteen issues), and with a limited distribution (some nine hundred copies), but nevertheless became well known in some circles in the Arabic-speaking world – though it is possible that it became better known in later years than it was at the time.

*Al-Urwa al-wuthqa* was published from a small room near the Place de la Madeleine. The costs of printing, and presumably also Muhammad Abduh's and Afghani's living expenses, were paid by sympathizers, including the Irish activist Wilfrid Blunt, an exiled general living in Italy, and the deposed khedive Ismail, with whom Ibrahim al-Muwaylihi was closely connected. Ismail routinely subsidized activities of this sort, as did other exiled princes. Slightly more than half the copies of *Al-Urwa al-wuthqa* were mailed to Egypt, and most of the remainder went to the Ottoman Empire – notably to Beirut and Istanbul. After a few issues, a British official in India reported that "Within the limits of its four pages it contains nothing that is not anti-English. The paper in my humble opinion is not fit to be allowed into India, although fortunately, there are not many in this country who read Arabic." The British in Egypt evidently came to a similar conclusion, since they prohibited the entry of further issues. It seems that at about this time *Al-Urwa al-wuthqa* also ran out of money.

## MUHAMMAD ABDUH AND WILFRID BLUNT

Wilfrid Blunt, who had first met Afghani and Muhammad Abduh in Egypt during the Urabi Revolt, remained interested in them in exile, partly because of his own continued efforts to lobby the British government – to which his wealth and family connections gave him good access – to modify its policy regarding Egypt, and partly because of a new interest in the Sudan. The collapse of Egyptian power in the Sudan that was caused by the British occupation of Egypt had permitted a successful uprising against Egyptian rule there. This was led by an unusual Sudanese Sufi, Muhammad Ahmad, who presented himself as the Mahdi – the "guided one" who is predicted by Muslim eschatology to come at the end of time and lead the Muslims in the final battle against Satan that is expected to precede the day of judgment. The Sudan was a major concern for the British public, since a half-hearted and poorly organized attempt to defeat the Mahdi had resulted in the isolation of one of the British public's greatest heroes, General Charles Gordon, under siege in Khartoum. Blunt was convinced that Afghani was in close contact with the Mahdi, which was not the case. Afghani evidently found Blunt's mistake useful.

Blunt visited Afghani in Paris. He described Muhammad Abduh at this time as "somewhat Europeanized already by a two months' stay in Paris. He had left off shaving his head, and wore a fez instead of a turban, which rather detracted from his dignity as shaykh, though he was still dressed in a respectable fur pelisse [cloak]." Muhammad Abduh's change of clothing may have indicated a change in the identity he wished to project, from Azhari to secular intellectual. Saad Zaghlul had made this change in 1880, dropping the religious title of shaykh as well as the turban, and adopting the secular title of *effendi* as well as the fez. Alternatively, it may have been for purely practical reasons. The fez was known to the French as standard modern Ottoman dress, and would have attracted somewhat less attention than a turban in the streets of Paris. It would also have been more useful in the rain. Afghani, however, continued to dress as a member of the ulema. Importantly for Muhammad Abduh's subsequent career, the change of headgear and identity was not permanent.

A further glimpse of the life that Muhammad Abduh was living in Paris is given by a discussion that Blunt observed with some visitors of his: "a Russian lady, an American philanthropist, and two young Bengalis who announced themselves as Theosophists" – that is, as followers of Helena Petrovna Blavatsky's Theosophical Society, the headquarters of which had been moved from New York to India in 1880–82. In Europe, the Theosophical Society was associated with spiritism and a post-Christian religiosity that drew on both Western esotericism and Hinduism. In India it was also associated with Indian nationalism. Whether Muhammad Abduh's relations with the Bengali Theosophists were based on a shared interest in nationalism or on a shared interest in alternative religion, then, is hard to say.

Muhammad Abduh's visitors expressed general sympathy with the Mahdi, but were worried about what they had heard of the Mahdi's views on the slave trade. Resistance to British and Egyptian attempts to end the slave trade in the Sudan were, in fact, one of the major reasons for support for the Mahdi, and the Mahdi had ended restrictions on the enslavement of non-Muslim Africans. According to Blunt, Muhammad Abduh "explained how much slaves gained among Mohammedans in exchange for their freedom." "This sent them away happy," wrote Blunt, "but the poor shaykh was put to his last shifts to hide his amusement." It is not clear what amused Muhammad Abduh most – the naivety of his visitors at accepting his rather weak justification for slavery, or the fact that he had been obliged to produce such a justification in the first place. Nothing else suggests that Muhammad Abduh was an enthusiast of slavery, a system that had been abolished in Egypt in 1877, though a few house slaves were still kept there until the end of the century.

The following month, Blunt arranged for Muhammad Abduh to visit London to assist him in his lobbying. Muhammad Abduh arrived in London in July 1884, and was taken by Blunt to the House of Commons, where he was presented as one of the leaders of the Egyptian National Party (which was no longer really the case). Blunt was aware of the importance of public relations, and persuaded Muhammad Abduh to wear for this visit "his blue jibbeh [gown] and white turban" – not the fez Muhammad Abduh had adopted in Paris. "He created quite a sensation in the lobby [of the House of Commons]," wrote Blunt with satisfaction. This is the occasion on which Muhammad Abduh was photographed, probably for the first time. The photograph in question, which shows a grave and handsome religious figure, has since become one of the two best-known photographs of Muhammad Abduh. Few realize that the location of the photograph is the House of Commons, or that Muhammad Abduh's religious robes had been pressed on him for the occasion by an Irishman.

Over the next few days, Muhammad Abduh met a range of British opposition politicians. He started with George Howard, later the Earl of Carlisle, an aristocratic Liberal MP who had traveled in Egypt but was perhaps more interested in art than politics. He was introduced to Charles Stewart Parnell, the great Irish nationalist leader, and to Lord Randolph Churchill, a leading opponent of Prime Minister William Gladstone (and the father of Winston Churchill). Finally, he met Henry Labouchere, a wealthy radical MP who specialized in attacking Gladstone for his Egyptian policy, and advocated a British withdrawal from all of Egypt save the Suez Canal. Labouchere was the politician Blunt most wanted Muhammad Abduh to meet. He tried to persuade Muhammad Abduh of the usefulness of what would later have been called a campaign of civil disobedience in Egypt – a refusal to pay taxes under British occupation. Muhammad Abduh did not like the idea. He responded that it was more likely to produce British annexation than British withdrawal.

In the event, there was never a tax strike, and Britain anyhow declared a protectorate over Egypt in 1914. Neither Blunt's nor Muhammad Abduh's activities in London had any significant consequences for either British or Egyptian politics. They must have had some consequences for Muhammad Abduh personally, though. At twenty-eight he had been in contact with the highest political levels of khedival Egypt. At thirty-five he experienced at first hand political levels of the British Empire that were important, if not the very highest. For most Egyptians, Britain was a monolithic and remote entity. Muhammad Abduh had seen that this was not the case. He had also experienced representative government in action, as well as read about it in theory.

While in London, Muhammad Abduh stayed at Blunt's house. Another guest at dinner one evening was Mirza Muhammad Baqir, a Persian friend of Afghani who knew English and Arabic. Baqir was unusual in having changed his religion twice – after converting from Islam to Christianity, he converted from Christianity back to Islam. Blunt records that during dinner Muhammad Abduh and Baqir discussed the nature of the Quran, Baqir arguing that it was "originally a book" and Muhammad Abduh arguing that it was "a compilation of oral sentences." Blunt understood that Muhammad Abduh was arguing for a more historical and less divine understanding of the origins of the Quran than Baqir was. It is possible, however, that Blunt had failed to recognize the ancient and intricate debate over whether the Quran was created in time, or was uncreated – that is, existing from all eternity, from before time. Muhammad Abduh may have been arguing against the standard Sunni position that the Quran existed through all eternity (was a book originally), and for the alternative position, generally held by the Shi'a, that the Quran was created. He did, in fact, express this view on a later occasion. In that case, however, Baqir would have been arguing for the Sunni position – which would be strange in a Persian, even one who had spent a period as a Christian. Whatever Muhammad Abduh was actually arguing in London, however, it is clear that he had been reflecting on the nature of God's revelation to humanity, and had perhaps come to conclusions which were unusual, either in Sunni terms or, perhaps, in Islamic terms.

## *AL-URWA AL-WUTHQA*

More important for history than meetings in London was the newspaper *Al-Urwa al-wuthqa*. It is generally agreed that most of *Al-Urwa al-wuthqa* was written by Muhammad Abduh. Since the positions it took coincide with those Afghani was then taking, however, the final responsibility for the views expressed in it must to some extent be shared between Muhammad Abduh and Afghani.

The basic line of *Al-Urwa al-wuthqa* was, somewhat surprisingly, support for the Ottoman sultan, Abd al-Hamid, as Caliph and leader of the Muslims worldwide, a role that Abd al-Hamid himself was promoting, using his religious role as Caliph to bolster his secular political role. This involved two significant shifts from the policy of nationalist constitutionalism followed by Afghani and Muhammad Abduh in Egypt. First, it required the abandonment of the earlier definition of the national community as being geographically based (for example, that of Egypt or India) and above religious divisions. Indian nationalists had generally condemned division along religious lines because it was necessary to form a common front against the British, and Afghani and Muhammad Abduh had previously taken a similar line with regard to Egypt, where the Coptic Christian and Jewish minorities constituted some one tenth of the population, and were especially significant because of their unusual prominence in commercial life, and – as we have seen – in journalism. "Can anyone doubt," asked Muhammad Abduh rhetorically while under arrest in Cairo, "that our struggle was a national one when men of all races and creeds – Muslims, Copts, and Jews – rushed to join it with enthusiasm?" A similar emphasis on cooperation across religious boundaries was later to be found in the case of the Wafd, the highly successful Egyptian nationalist party formed by Saad Zaghlul after the First World War.

Second, the line of *Al-Urwa al-wuthqa* required the abandonment of the fight against tyranny. Abd al-Hamid, known in opposition circles as "the red" for the quantity of blood he had on his hands, had become sultan in 1876 with the support of a constitutionalist movement similar to that which supported the khedive Tawfiq in Egypt, but had quickly moved against the constitutionalists, suspending the constitution and later killing the leader of the constitutionalist party. He then instituted an absolute autocracy along the most modern lines, complete with strict censorship, a ubiquitous secret police, and a system of denunciations that anticipated Stalin's. By the time of his final deposition from effective power by a military coup in 1908, he had become so unpopular that the news of the coup was greeted by dancing in the streets of major cities across his empire.

The support of Afghani and Muhammad Abduh for Abd al-Hamid was clearly opportunistic. Blunt reports that Muhammad Abduh spoke with feeling against Abd al-Hamid and the injustices of his rule in Syria in late March 1884, when *Al-Urwa al-wuthqa* had already started publication. The decision to support Abd al-Hamid was probably Afghani's, since Afghani had written in 1882, in an émigré newspaper published in London (*Al-Nahla*, "The bee"), of the caliphate as "al-urwa al-wuthqa," the firmest bond to which Muslims might hold, ascribing the British invasion of Egypt to British fear that Muslims might rally round the Ottoman sultan and so threaten Britain's hold on India. In an 1883 article in *Al-Basir* ("Insight"), a Syrian émigré newspaper published in Paris, Afghani argued that what was urgently needed was unity among Eastern peoples, and that attacks on the sultan might weaken this unity. If the Ottoman government were overthrown, individual Eastern peoples would be defenseless against Europe. Reforms could come later. Although in the event the Eastern unity for which Afghani hoped never materialized (save perhaps in the form of the Bandung Conference of 1955), events after the final collapse of the Ottoman Empire in 1918 proved him right: the overthrow of the Ottoman government and state did indeed result in the European occupation of almost the whole Arab world.

A similar logic was expressed by Muhammad Abduh in an interview by Blunt, published in English in the *Pall Mall Gazette*. Before 1882, Muhammad Abduh explained,

> We wished to break down the tyranny of our rulers; we complained of the Turks as foreigners; we wished to improve ourselves politically, and to advance as the nations of Europe have advanced on the path of liberty. Now we know that there are worse evils than despotism and worse enemies than the Turks.

The context makes clear that the "worse evils" are foreign occupation, and that the "worse enemies" are the British.

Whether the support for Islamic nationalism – that is, for a definition of the community based on religion rather than geography – was also opportunist is not clear. One of the benefits of religion expounded in Afghani's 1881 *Haqiqat-i mazhab-i naichun* was national and social solidarity, so it is possible that Afghani had indeed changed his mind on this point.

Abduh too seems to have changed his mind, writing in favor of the religious community rather than the national one, and also – importantly – rather than the racial one. Since the horrors of Hitler's concentration camps, analyses framed in terms of racial communities have become unacceptable. During the nineteenth century, however, the ideas that were ultimately developed into Nazi racism were not only widespread but generally considered quite acceptable, as is indicated by Renan's analysis of the relationship between Islam and science in terms of differences between the Aryan and Semitic races, explained during a lecture at the Sorbonne. Afghani rejected this type of analysis in his response to Renan, but many Persians – whose language was undoubtedly of Aryan rather than Semitic origin — enthusiastically embraced such ideas, which were generally flattering to them. Since there was no possible way of arguing that Arabic or ancient Egyptian were anything but Semitic, however, there was no way in which Arabs or Egyptians could take advantage of these ideas. An analysis that stressed religion rather than race, then, had clear attractions.

Apart from the villainy of the British, the central arguments developed in *Al-Urwa al-wuthqa* were the importance of Muslim solidarity and the need for Muslims to adhere to "true" Islam. A favorite quotation from the Quran was the verse already used by Afghani at the end of his *Haqiqat-i mazhab-i naichun*, "Verily, God does not change the state of a people until they change themselves inwardly." This sentence (from Q. 13:11) had generally been understood to mean the opposite of what Afghani and Muhammad Abduh took it to mean. For most Sunnis, it meant that God does not deprive a people of His grace unless they have altered the state of their souls through an act of disobedience, but that when this happened "if God wills evil for a people there is no-one who can avert it, nor have they any protector save Him," as the verse concludes. The Quran is full of stories of peoples who turned from God and suffered accordingly, from the time of Noah, when general disobedience resulted in the Great Flood. Anyone who knows the Quran is inevitably very familiar with the point that disobedience results in punishment, for peoples on earth as well as for individuals after death. It is not hard to conclude from this that punishment indicates disobedience, and thus to proceed to the further point – developed by Afghani and Muhammad Abduh – that obedience will lift punishment. This view has since become very widely accepted among Muslims, and is still frequently expressed today.

As Muhammad Abduh wrote,

> Nations have not fallen from their greatness, nor have their names been wiped off the slate of existence, except after they have departed from those laws which God prescribed ... Ruin overtook [previous,

now vanished, nations] because they turned astray from the laws of justice and the path of insight and wisdom ... and chose to live in falsehood rather than die in the aid of truth.

The varieties of disobedience that Muhammad Abduh emphasized were generally social or political rather than religious or spiritual, however – as one might expect in a newspaper with a political agenda. He drew attention to the failure of Muslims in general to ponder over the word of God as required by Quran 23:68, and of failing to act with justice and kindness, as required by Quran 16:90. He also drew attention to the requirement in Quran 3:103 that Muslims should not be divided, and the requirement in Quran 60:1 that Muslims should not make friends of those who were their own enemies and the enemies of God (i.e. unbelievers such as the British). Muslim rulers were chided for exulting in the luxuries of life contrary to Quran 28:58, and for failing to use mutual consultation (*shura*), as enjoined by Quran 3:159 and Quran 42:38.

This highly political understanding of the essentials of Islam was not put in one paragraph as it has been above, but results from a condensation of the Quranic quotations most often used in *Al-Urwa al-wuthqa*. The point, however, is clear. Muhammad Abduh was not stressing the aspects of Islam that the vast majority of preachers of the time would have stressed: acceptance of the will of God in one's heart, and compliance with the laws of God in one's life. Instead, he was stressing the aspects of Islam that fitted, or could be made to fit, his and Afghani's political program: intellectual and moral reform of the individual, solidarity against European imperialism, and an end to despotic government (with an exemption for Sultan Abd al-Hamid).

Muhammad Abduh's interpretations of the meaning of the Quranic verses he selected were novel, as he would have been the first to appreciate, given his Azhari training. Quran 16:90 was generally understood in the ethical sense in which Muhammad Abduh interpreted it, as requiring justice and kindness, and Quran 3:103 could be stretched without too much difficulty to cover political unity. Quran 23:68, however, which Muhammad Abduh interpreted to require thought about the meaning of the Quran, was generally understood to emphasize that many of those who would receive divine punishment would lack the excuse that they had had no opportunity to appreciate the message of the Quran, not to encourage reflection and reason. The prohibition on making friends with unbelievers in Quran 60:1 was generally understood to have applied only to relations between the Muslims at the time of the Prophet and those unbelievers in Mecca who at first opposed the Prophet, not to apply more generally. Quran 3:159 was generally considered to have referred to the need for consultation between the Prophet and certain of his followers, not more generally, and Quran 42:38 was thought to encourage consultation between pious individuals, not between ruler and ruled. That few religious scholars would have agreed with his interpretations did not worry Muhammad Abduh, however. *Al-Urwa al-wuthqa* attacked the whole class of the ulema, who had failed to maintain unity among Muslims.

Muhammad Abduh also advanced an unusual understanding of jihad in *Al-Urwa al-wuthqa*. Islamic jurisprudence makes a distinction between communal and individual duties. The study of classical Arabic grammar, for example, is a communal duty – so long as enough Muslims are engaged in it, knowledge which is essential to proper analysis of the Quran remains current. Prayer, in contrast, is an individual duty – each and every Muslim must pray. Jihad had generally been understood as a communal duty – like the study of Arabic grammar, the main point was that enough Muslims should be engaged in it. This is the view of warfare taken by most societies: what matters is to have enough soldiers, not that every single person should become a soldier. Jihad became an individual duty, just as prayer was, only when the enemy had entered Muslim territory. Muhammad Abduh, however, argued that jihad to keep Muslim lands under Muslim control was always an individual duty. This argument (which was also made by Osama bin Laden in 1998) has major implications, since it takes control of warfare out of the hands of rulers, and makes individuals responsible for it, on their own private initiative. In the event, it was not until many years after Muhammad Abduh's death that individual jihadism became popular.

In *Al-Urwa al-wuthqa*, then, Muhammad Abduh was making use of the Quran to endorse his and Afghani's political and social positions. Not only were the conclusions drawn different from those usually drawn, but a different methodology was used. The established method of Quran interpretation, as learned by Muhammad Abduh in Tanta and at the Azhar, was the painstaking attempt to discover the original and true meaning of the divinely revealed text, using finely honed tools of etymological and grammatical analysis, and with reference to allied texts such as those *hadith* which explained the circumstances in which a verse had been revealed. This, for example, was the basis on which the prohibition on making friends with non-Muslims had been understood to be restricted to the time of the Prophet. Muhammad Abduh, however, was not trying to elucidate meaning, but to develop possible meanings – and if this meant that allied texts and existing understandings had to be ignored, so be it.

Muhammad Abduh also chose to ignore his own interpretation of Quran 60:1, against making friends with unbelievers. Not only had he been on friendly terms with Christians and at least one Jew (Sannua) in Cairo while fighting khedival despotism, but he was in a friendly alliance with Wilfrid Blunt at the very time at which he was promoting the idea that Quran 60:1 prohibited such friendships. If Muhammad Abduh had been engaged in elucidating the meaning of the divine revelation, this would have been hypocrisy. Since Muhammad Abduh was engaged in politics, however, it would have been reasonable to make a distinction between what was the right approach for the Muslim world as a whole, and what was appropriate for individuals in positions such as his own. The unbelievers he was making friends with were not imperialists or despots, but their opponents.

*Al-Urwa al-wuthqa* may have been small and short lived, and had a limited distribution, but it was highly innovative. A fuller study of the Ottoman and Indian émigré presses of the period than currently exists would be required to establish to what extent the ideas and perspectives it advanced were truly original, but nothing quite like it had been seen before in Arabic. During the 1870s, Afghani and his circle had invented liberal nationalist political journalism in Egypt; in 1884, Afghani and Abduh invented what would now be called radical Islamist journalism in Arabic, including the use of Islam for political ends.

# BEIRUT

*Al-Urwa al-wuthqa* published its final issue in October 1884, either because it had lost its main readership when the British had forbidden its import into Egypt and India, or because it had run out of money, or perhaps for both reasons. In November or December of that year, Muhammad Abduh left Paris for Tunis, which had recently become a French protectorate, on a fundraising trip. On December 24, he reported to Afghani that while he had failed to raise any money, he had established a local branch of Al-urwa al-wuthqa (the group, not the newspaper). He added that people in Tunis were not aware that the newspaper had stopped publishing.

This letter from Muhammad Abduh to Afghani is the last communication known to have passed between the two men. It marks the end not only of what was without doubt the most important relationship in Muhammad Abduh's life, but also of Muhammad Abduh's political activism. In 1885 Muhammad Abduh left Tunis, but for Syria, where he began a second – and very different – phase of his career.

## THE BREAK WITH AFGHANI

Exactly what happened in Tunis is not known. The cause of the break with Afghani does not seem to have been on the latter's side, however, since his subsequent career followed on already established lines. He spent part of 1885 in London with Blunt, where he tried to bolster British support for the Ottomans against Russia, at that point the major threat to the Ottoman Empire. The relationship with Blunt ceased after an argument at Blunt's house between Afghani and "two of his Oriental friends" which grew so heated that they "ended by beating each other over the heads with umbrellas." Blunt asked all concerned to leave. Afghani proceeded to Tehran, then to Russia, then back to Tehran, and finally – in 1891 – to Ottoman Iraq, from where he resumed his struggle against European power and despotic rule, this time that of Shah Nasr al-Din of Persia. He was partly responsible for one of the most effective political actions of the period, a mass boycott of tobacco in Persia which forced the shah to cancel a concession that had been given to a British firm, and which also demonstrated the potential power of the general public and the weakness of the shah's regime. He may also have been responsible for the assassination of the shah in 1896. He died in 1897, under house arrest in Istanbul.

Since Afghani's political positions and activities remained consistent while Muhammad Abduh's changed, the implication is that the cause of the break was that Muhammad Abduh came to reject Afghani's approach. He later said that "the interests of the Muslims have become inextricably interwoven with the interests of the Europeans in every country in the world," and clearly came to the conclusion that cooperation with Europe would produce better results than confrontation. Perhaps he remembered Guizot's version of the effect of the crusades on Europe: more important than Europe's initial military victory or her final military defeat was the long-term impact on Europe of the encounter with a superior civilization. At any rate, cooperation rather then confrontation was henceforth to be Muhammad Abduh's principle.

Muhammad Abduh was not the only Arab opponent of European imperialism who abandoned the struggle as impossible. The former leader of the Algerian resistance to France, the Amir Abd al-Qadir, was one of the many others who reached similar conclusions. Ahmad Khan in India, whose views on polygamy were echoed by Muhammad Abduh but whose "naturism" had been condemned by

Afghani, was another. Although Arab nationalists of the twentieth century would condemn this approach as surrender and collaboration, by 1884 attempts at armed resistance to European states had all been comprehensively defeated, and no significant change in power relations could be foreseen. European dominance then seemed so great, and so well established, that a decision to abandon confrontation is certainly understandable. In the event, European power tottered after the First World War and crumbled after the Second World War; the Persian tobacco boycott and the assassination of 1896 came to be seen by some as part of the story that ended in the humiliation of the West by the Iranian Revolution. Events, then, might be understood as vindicating Afghani, not Muhammad Abduh. Those events, however, lay far in the future.

Ibrahim al-Muwaylihi, who had been with Afghani and Muhammad Abduh in Paris as well as during their attempt to promote the "national plan" in Egypt under Ismail, also broke with Afghani at about this time. However, he broke with Muhammad Abduh too. He suggested that Muhammad Abduh had been more successful in raising cash in Tunis than he had admitted, and had kept it for himself, but this is unlikely. Embezzlement is not unheard of among émigrés, but nothing else that is known of Muhammad Abduh, or even has been alleged about him, suggests dishonesty. Al-Muwaylihi, on the other hand, was becoming known for slandering his enemies.

The break between Muhammad Abduh and Afghani is a dramatic one, and cannot be explained with certainty. It probably resulted from a reassessment on Muhammad Abduh's part of what was and what was not possible in the circumstances of the times. There may, however, have been some other cause about which we do not know.

## IN SEARCH OF AN OCCUPATION

Muhammad Abduh returned to Beirut, where he had friends from his first period in exile, only two years before. His first wife had died, leaving him with a baby daughter, and he married the niece of Muhyi al-Din Bey Humada, the reformist mayor of Beirut with whom he had stayed on first arriving in Beirut from Cairo. His new wife's father, Saad al-Din, was also a modernist reformer, a founding member of Beirut's Society of Arts, the origin of the later – and very famous – Muslim Benevolent Society.

Presumably through these connections, Muhammad Abduh found employment at the Sultaniyya, a modern school that had recently been established (in 1883) to compete with the many European schools that had opened in Beirut. It emphasized both modern sciences and religion – Islam for most, and Christianity for some – and was in some ways the counterpart of Ahmad Khan's Muhammadan Anglo-Oriental College, save that it admitted Christians as well as Muslims. It was attended by the children of the Syrian elite: no fewer than seven members of Jerusalem's leading family, the Husaynis, went to the Sultaniyya, for example.

At the Sultaniyya, Muhammad Abduh taught history, which he had also taught in Cairo using the works of Ibn Khaldun and François Guizot, as well as *tawhid*, theology, a task for which he was qualified by his Azhari training. The turban of the religious shaykh, then, was to replace the fez that he had worn in Paris. His lectures on *tawhid* were recorded, possibly by the brother of his new father-in-law, and later published. They are discussed below. He also taught some classic literary texts, notably the *Diwan al-hamasa* of the celebrated ninth-century poet Abu Tammam Habib ibn Aws al-Ta'i, and the *Maqamat* of the tenth-century author Badi al-Zaman al-Hamadhani, an almost unique example of early Arabic fiction based on the adventures of a likeable rogue, Abu al-Fath al-Iskandari. Finally, he taught – and edited – the *Nahj al-balagha* ("The peak of eloquence"), traditionally attributed to the Imam Ali ibn Abi Talib. He may have taught this work for its literary value, but it was also a religious text – and associated more with Shi'i Islam than with Sunni Islam, suggesting that Muhammad Abduh's own education at the hands of Afghani continued to exert an influence. The other works suggest a commitment to an Arabic literary renaissance, for which many progressives in Beirut were then also working.

Two documents from this period suggest an attempt to enter Ottoman public life, one addressed to the Ottoman governor of Beirut, and the other addressed to an education reform commission then sitting in Istanbul under the Shaykh al-Islam, the highest official in the Ottoman religious hierarchy. The latter document starts with the somewhat excessive protestations of devotion to the sultan that were then customary. The topic of both documents was the improvement of Muslim education in the face of competition from foreign schools, a subject about which Muhammad Abduh could write with some authority, given his experience at the Sultaniyya. This was an issue that preoccupied the Ottoman elite, concerned that future Ottoman citizens were being educated to be more loyal to foreign countries than to their own, and were being exposed to dangerous foreign ideas, if not actually led to convert to Christianity – which was, of course, the ultimate objective of many of the schools in question, the majority of which were run by Christian missionaries. Thirty-three unlicensed American Protestant schools in Syria were closed down during 1885, but the Ottomans faced a difficult task. In 1888 (the closest year for which we have figures) the Ottoman budget for education in Beirut was 1,200,000 piasters, half of which was allocated to capital expenditure. The French government budget for subsidizing French-language schools in Beirut was 460,000 piasters, i.e. three quarters of the total Ottoman budget available for current expenditure. In addition to French schools, there were also British, American, Italian, and German schools, not to mention local private Christian schools that were often assisted by foreigners.

Despite the hostility to foreign Christian schools which is clear in these documents, Muhammad Abduh himself continued to have good relations with Christians. In Cairo he had been on good terms with Christian members of the Afghani group; in Beirut he went beyond personal relations and entered what would today be called inter-religious dialog. It was probably during this period – though possibly during his earlier period in Beirut in 1883 – that he was in contact with an English clergyman, the Reverend Isaac Taylor, who had an interest in Islam. In a private correspondence, Muhammad

Abduh told Taylor that in his view Islam and Christianity agreed on far more than they disagreed, and that although both religions had departed from what they were meant to be, "true religion shines through all the religions." The day would soon come, thought Muhammad Abduh, when "perfect knowledge" would reign among men, and – according to one version – "the two great religions, Christianity and Islam, would respect each other and take each other's hand." According to Taylor's own version, the expectation was not just that Christianity and Islam would come to appreciate each other, but that there would emerge "one pure faith which all will be able to accept."

The view that there had once been, and might again be, a single pure and universal religion was not one that Taylor himself shared, but was not unusual in the 1880s. It is to be found, for example, in the writings of Helena Blavatsky, founder of the Theosophical Society, and this may have been where Muhammad Abduh had taken it from, given that Blunt reported finding two Bengali Theosophists in Muhammad Abduh's company in Paris. Similar views were held by the Baha'is, a group of Persian origin that finally developed into a new religion, with which Muhammad Abduh was also in contact. Though not unusual in "advanced" circles in Paris, however, such views were then (as now) highly unusual in the Arab world, and Muhammad Abduh is not known ever to have expressed them in public. He is, however, reported to have attempted to establish in Beirut a society for uniting Muslims, Christians, and Jews, in cooperation with Mirza Muhammad Baqir, the Persian friend of Afghani with whom he had debated the nature of the Quran over dinner at Blunt's house in London. Nothing seems to have come of this society, with which Taylor may also have been involved.

A charming story ascribes Muhammad Abduh's later departure from Beirut to his conversion of Taylor to Islam. According to this story, after Taylor addressed a meeting of clergymen in London, these clergymen complained to Queen Victoria, who asked Sultan Abd al-Hamid about Muhammad Abduh. Sultan Abd al-Hamid was concerned that if Queen Victoria became Muslim, she might replace him as Caliph of all the Muslims, and so – for safety's sake – ordered Muhammad Abduh expelled from Beirut.

Taylor did indeed gain some fame for speaking in favor of Islam, but not exactly in complimentary terms. In 1887, he addressed a Church Congress (not in London, but in Wolverhampton, a city in the Midlands) on the subject of "Mohamedanism." Islam, he argued, was "eminently adapted to be a civilizing and elevating religion for barbarous tribes," even though it was "quite unfitted for the higher races." That Taylor's speech caused outrage (and may even have come to the attention of Queen Victoria, who presumably read the newspapers) was not just because of Taylor's rather limited praise for Islam, or even for the defense of slavery he delivered in that connection, but also because of his related argument that "the 'Christian ideal' [was] unintelligible to savages." This implied that the Church's overseas missionary activities were pointless and misguided, and was probably a major cause of the uproar his speech caused.

Muhammad Abduh's correspondence with Taylor confirms the picture suggested by earlier glimpses of his religious views, of a man whose understanding of Islam was highly unusual. It does not suggest an atheist, though atheism was to be found in Beirut. Adib Ishaq, the Christian member of the Afghani group who had edited *Misr* and *Al-Tijara* in Cairo and had been in Paris when Muhammad Abduh arrived there, had died in Beirut at the age of twenty-eight, while Muhammad Abduh was still in Paris. Known for his dissolute lifestyle, and having refused the attentions of a priest on his deathbed, Ishaq was initially refused a Christian burial by the Church, on the grounds that he was an atheist.

## *RISALAT AL-TAWHID*

Muhammad Abduh's lectures from the Sultaniyya were published as *Risalat al-tawhid* ("Essay on theology"), and are often called in English "The Theology of Unity" – *tawhid* means "unity" as well as, approximately, "theology." This is now Muhammad Abduh's most famous work, but its fame is mostly posthumous. It was published in a small edition in Cairo in 1897, and seems then to have attracted little attention. It was republished after his death, in 1908, and since then has been frequently reprinted, as well as translated into French, English, and other languages. The 1908 edition, however, differed in several ways from the 1897 edition, as the editor removed or toned down Muhammad Abduh's more unusual passages. The comments below relate to the original edition.

Despite its title, *Risalat al-tawhid* is not really about theology. It is about Islam and Muslims in the modern world, and in effect argues for an Islamic Enlightenment or an Islamic Reformation. It is a religious work, then, if not a theological one. It is addressed to the sort of Muslim who Muhammad Abduh was teaching at the Sultaniyya – Muslims who knew European languages, studied modern European philosophy and science and history, and who needed to find a way of being progressive and rationalist and Muslim at the same time. Otherwise, as Muhammad Abduh wrote, some Muslims might look at the ignorance of the Muslim ulema and turn away from Islam, regarding it as "a kind of old *thobe* in which it is embarrassing to appear" – a *thobe* being the old-fashioned robe still worn by the poor, but no longer used by the educated. Ishaq was probably not the only atheist in Beirut. His atheism became generally known only as a result of the Church's initial refusal to bury him; the atheism of others probably remained concealed.

Muhammad Abduh was not the only teacher at the Sultaniyya who addressed modern Muslims. One of the directors of the school, Husayn al-Jisr, also wrote on Darwin, in his *Risala hamadiyya fi haqiqat al-diyana al-islamiyya wa haqiqat al-shari'a al-muhammidiyya* ("Essay on the truth of the Islamic faith and the truth of the Muhammadan sharia"). Al-Jisr argued that Islam does not contradict science and that "so long as you believe that God is the creator, whether or not you believe that all of His creatures were created at once or gradually in evolutionary stages, your faith as a Muslim remains uncorrupted." *Risalat al-tawhid* may be unusual in an Islamic context, then, but was less unusual in the context of the Sultaniyya.

*Risalat al-tawhid* starts somewhat philosophically. After arguing that Islam was at its origin identical with reason, even if this relationship was later destroyed, Muhammad Abduh deduces the existence of God from the need for a prior cause, and argues that God can be known rationally. Reason cannot penetrate the divine essence, however, which is one reason for revealed religion.

Moving from philosophy to sociology, Muhammad Abduh argues that although humans – who have free will – could in theory act rationally, judging the value of acts on the basis of their consequences, in practice they often act foolishly or ignorantly, once again giving rise to a need for revealed religion to guide them. Not only is revealed religion necessary, but the revelation of religion through human agents is also possible. Just as some men are cleverer than others and grasp immediately things that it takes other men ages to understand, some "see the things of God as if by natural vision." These are the prophets.

Religion deals with things of the spirit, not with everyday things – it has no bearing on astronomy, for example, although it may establish general principles in such areas as economic life. Religion has certainly led to social discord, but actually has a positive and constructive social function, especially for the masses, whom it makes content, industrious, submissive, and respectful. The argument here echoes Afghani's emphasis on the social utility of religion in his *Haqiqat-i mazhab-i naichun*. It is not so much that religion is justified by its social usefulness, as that it is not to be condemned as a social evil.

After thus establishing the necessity, possibility, and positive social function of religion, Muhammad Abduh turns to the case of Islam. The Prophet Muhammad came at a time of general collapse and disarray, bringing arguments that convinced people by their rational force, and a Quran than convinced people by its logic. The result was Islam, which freed humanity from irrationality and exploitation, and provided the basis of civilization, a pattern for the good life. This might be difficult to believe, looking at Muslims now, and seeing their ignorance, laziness, dishonesty, and disunity, not to mention the way that they lack all independence, following tyrants and enslaving others. This, however, is because of what happened afterwards. Theological disputes first led Muslims to turn away from reason, making room for the adoption of strange and false beliefs, which finally led to a situation where "complete intellectual confusion afflicted the Muslims under ignorant rulers." However, a return to the true Islam of the first Muslims, the *salaf* who had been cited by the earlier reformers that Muhammad Abduh may have encountered in Damascus, might once again establish a rational civilization, and a good life.

Muhammad Abduh was more concerned to explain and promote his version of "true" Islam than to justify it. Earlier ulema had devoted much time to questions of interpretative methodology, on the basis that the right methodology would lead to the right interpretation. Most classic methodologies gave equal weight to the Quran and to the *hadith*, the reports of the words and actions of the Prophet Muhammad. Some Indian reformers – including the followers of Ahmad Khan whom Afghani had attacked in *Haqiqat-i mazhab-i naichun* – had proposed greater reliance on the Quran than on the *hadith*, partly as a result of doubts raised by European Orientalist scholarship concerning the authenticity of many of the *hadith*. Muhammad Abduh did not spend much time on these methodological questions, but he too preferred to emphasize the Quran. He argued, relatively briefly, that the *hadith* should be used much more carefully than was generally the case. Only those whose authenticity was beyond all doubt should be accepted, while ensuring that they either made sense or were understood in a way that made sense.

According to Muhammad Abduh, a careful reading of the Quran shows that men are free and equal. Man was liberated by true Islam "from the bonds that tied him to the will of others" – of rulers and masters, of those who pretend to represent God – and also from the illusion that divine power might be inherent in "tombs, stones, trees, [or] stars." True Islam asks man to work according to his abilities, and gives him the fruit of his labors. It forbids *taqlid* (strict adherence to precedent), and encourages the use of reason, giving man "independence of will and independence of opinion and thought," the very qualities that "one of the Western sages" (in fact, Guizot, though he is not named) found to be the basis of European civilization. True Islam also includes rational worship. Islam makes clear the nature of man and society, showing the courses of action that lead to unfortunate consequences for individuals, and the transgressions that lead to disaster for societies. The *salaf* lived by these principles, and prospered. Others foolishly supposed that prosperity could be achieved by prayer and intercession, and did not prosper. Finally, Islam gives the poor some right to the property of the rich, eliminating social envy, and forbids the origins of several major social evils – alcohol, gambling, and usury.

Certain major misconceptions about Islam are also addressed. One concerns violence, a major issue in the nineteenth century just as it is today. As well as arguing that the revelation of the Prophet Muhammad triumphed by virtue of its logic, Muhammad Abduh specifically denies any use of force – by avoiding all mention of the armed struggle between the Prophet and the early Muslims on the one hand, and the reluctant polytheists of Mecca on the other. Although he could not avoid reference to the conquest of half the Byzantine Empire and the whole of the Persian Empire by the early Muslims, he attempted to present these as acts of self-defense: the Byzantines and the Persians attacked first, and once conquered were treated with exceptional kindness and fairness. Muslim fighting during the crusades was also defensive, and was anyhow very much to the benefit of Europe, which discovered true civilization in the Muslim world – a discovery which gave rise to the Reformation, which not only advanced European civilization, but also gave rise to Protestantism, a somewhat Islamized (because more rational) form of Christianity.

Another misconception that is addressed is "oriental fatalism," which many Europeans saw as one of the main causes of the backwardness of the Muslim world. Muhammad Abduh does not disagree that fatalism causes backwardness, and that it is prevalent in the Orient. His argument is that fatalism is not Islamic. He argues that in reality human actions are "derived" from God, "building on capacities given ... by God." For example, it is medicine, given by God, that cures disease – not, by implication, God. God can certainly do things beyond what man can do with what God has already given man, but man has to use what God has given him first.

In some ways, *Risalat al-tawhid* is more about Muslim history and society than about Islam. It deals with issues such as liberty, independent reasoning, and self-help that were never the concern of the traditional ulema, often using concepts derived from nineteenth-century European thought (especially Guizot) that Muslims of earlier centuries would have had difficulty in comprehending. The contrast between Muhammad Abduh's work and traditional Muslim scholarship is absolute. The discussions of the necessity of first causes and of predestination use familiar terms and concepts, but to very different ends. The familiar methodology of painstaking exegesis of Quranic texts and of the *hadith* to derive detailed rules of religious practice is entirely absent – indeed, detailed rules of practice, the main concern of Islamic scholarship for a millennium, are themselves absent, replaced by statements of general principle. *Risalat al-tawhid*, then, is a thoroughly modern work.

*Risalat al-tawhid* is well and clearly written, and generally convincing, even though its arguments are sometimes weak. The claim that force played no part in the early history of Islam, for example, is simply a distortion of history. The claim that the Quran convinced by its logic depends on understanding the word *balagha* as meaning "logic." The Quran's *balagha* had always been accepted as a proof of its authenticity, and this is Muhammad Abduh's starting point. The term *balagha* does include a sense of "logic," but is generally translated into English not as "logic" but as "eloquence," which is actually closer to the meaning of the Arabic. Stylistic perfection is an important element of *balagha*, for example. Similarly, Muhammad Abduh asserts that "all Muslims" are agreed that some things can only be understood by reason, and that while some things may be beyond our understanding, nothing in religion is against reason. It would have been more accurate to say that many Persian Shi'i scholars were agreed on this – most Sunni scholars of the time would have flatly disagreed, and to ascribe the view to "all Muslims," today as in 1885, is contrary to reality. Perhaps Muhammad Abduh's weakest argument, however, comes in his case for the possibility of prophecy. If a sick person has visions, he asks, why should a prophet not have divine visions? This comparison really works rather better as a condemnation of religion than as a defense of it.

It is interesting to see how Muhammad Abduh deals with the relationship between religions, given the remarkable views on this topic that he expressed in his letter to Taylor. Rather as he did with Taylor, he argues in *Risalat al-tawhid* for there being a single true religion which emphasizes the existence of one God who should alone be worshiped, and stresses the need to obey certain rules for the general benefit of humanity. The differences between religions, however, are explained somewhat differently – in terms of different developmental stages requiring different types of religion. He avoids a classic evolutionary model, using instead the image of a child growing to maturity. He also rejects racial explanations of development, and reverses the racial and religious hierarchy that Taylor and many others then accepted. In humanity's infancy, according to Muhammad Abduh, religion consisted of clear commands of the sort that parents use with small children – the reference is clearly to Judaism, though Judaism is not mentioned by name, and echoes one of Afghani's points in the *Journal des débats* in 1883. In humanity's adolescence, a new religion that appealed to human hearts was needed, and so came Christianity. Finally, when humanity came of age, there came at last a religion that addressed reason: Islam. This is not an argument that would have appealed to Taylor. That Muhammad Abduh was presenting two different views on the same topic almost simultaneously suggests a care to adjust the message to the audience that borders on excessive flexibility.

The prescriptions of *Risalat al-tawhid* have struck some later commentators as overemphasizing the moral elements of reform, and underemphasizing the economic and technological elements that are the focus of today's development experts. Recent scholarly explanations of the European prosperity and power that Muhammad

Abduh evidently hoped to emulate focus not on morality but on demography, capital formation, trade, and industrialization. It should be noted, however, that European observers of the nineteenth century focused less on these factors than on precisely the type of moral factor that interested Muhammad Abduh. Europeans were seen as industrious, organized, and progressive, and non-Europeans as lazy, disorganized, and fatalistic. Muhammad Abduh, then, focused on much the same factors as his contemporaries did. Less moralistic versions of this approach are still found today, for example in the section of development studies which focuses on the impact of culture.

The lectures on which *Risalat al-tawhid* is based presumably went down well at the Sultaniyya. They presented an Islam that was anything but an embarrassing old *thobe*. Instead, it became a religion that was not only compatible with progress and progressive values, but which was actually in some ways more suitable for the modern age than the Christianity of the Europeans.

*Risalat al-tawhid* can be seen as the manifesto of modernist Islam. It draws on Guizot, and on views of progress that Muhammad Abduh had first acquired as a student of Afghani's, and that he had then refined on the basis of his experiences in Cairo, Paris, and London. In some ways it echoes the vision of "true" Islam that he had presented in the pages of *Al-Urwa al-wuthqa*, but without the radical political agenda that was found in that newspaper. It is also a complete vision, one that is mature as well as daring. Muhammad Abduh was thirty-six years old when he gave the lectures in question.

# 6

# THE RETURN TO EGYPT

Although Muhammad Abduh was well established in Beirut, he was not happy there. The Syrians "are not like my own people," he wrote, "and a day spent here is not like a day spent at home." Muhammad Abduh was an Egyptian, and wanted to return to Egypt. In 1888, this is what he did.

The Egypt to which he returned was very different from the Egypt he had left six years before. The British occupation that started as a response to the Urabi Revolt had become permanent, and although in theory Egypt remained an autonomous province of the Ottoman Empire under the hereditary rule of the khedive, in practice real power lay with Sir Evelyn Baring, the British consul-general and "agent" from 1883 until 1907. Baring, later ennobled as Lord Cromer (by which name he is better known), was the son of a member of the British parliament from a family of bankers, and had first come to Egypt as the British representative on the Commission of Inquiry established in response to the financial crisis of the 1870s. After spending three years in charge of the finances of the British government of India, he returned to Egypt in 1883 to supervise the evacuation of British troops, but instead stayed on to reorganize Egyptian finances – a task which extended first to the reorganization of the Egyptian economy and then to the reorganization of the entire Egyptian government. The full evacuation of British troops did not happen until after the Second World War. Baring's power derived from his control of finances and from the presence of British troops, and operated through the appointment of British "advisers" to various government departments. Although in theory these officials answered to the khedive, who paid their salaries, in practice they reported to Baring.

It was Baring who enabled Muhammad Abduh to return to Egypt, by pressing the khedive to pardon him and restore his employment in the Egyptian government service. The absence of employment was presumably what had been keeping Muhammad Abduh in Syria, since his term of exile from Egypt had expired at the end of 1885, and in theory he could have returned home then. It is not entirely clear how Baring had heard of him, but it is possible that he had read and liked a proposal for educational reform in Egypt that Muhammad Abduh had written in Beirut, rather as he had written proposals on the same topic for the Ottoman government. Muhammad Abduh hoped to return to teaching at the Dar al-Ulum, presumably intending to continue the classes he had been giving at the Sultaniyya in Beirut, but the khedive was unwilling to allow this, presumably because he still saw Muhammad Abduh as politically dangerous on the basis of his activities before and during the Urabi Revolt. Muhammad Abduh was instead appointed a judge in the National Court of First Instance in the provincial town of Banha, halfway between Cairo and Tanta, the town where he had run away from school at sixteen. This was a minor position, but at least it paid a salary that he could live off, and was in Egypt.

## THE NATIONAL COURTS

Egypt had three parallel judicial systems. The oldest of these was the Sharia Court system, which had existed from time immemorial, applying Islamic law and staffed by ulema. The second system, of so-called Judicial Councils, had been established in 1848 to apply administrative regulations and to act as special criminal courts, and was staffed by government officials. The third system was the Mixed Court system, established in 1875 to apply a civil code on the French model, and staffed partly by European and partly by Egyptian judges.

The Mixed Courts had jurisdiction over all cases involving Europeans, even if only one party to a dispute was a European. In 1882, the Judicial Council system was replaced by a system of National Courts, and this was the system in which Muhammad Abduh was appointed a judge. The National Courts were intended to apply modern codes similar to those used by the Mixed Courts, and took over much of the jurisdiction of the Sharia Courts, which were left only family and inheritance law, and made subordinate to the Ministry of Justice. The National Courts – as they were called in Arabic – were at the time known in English as the Native Courts.

It seems a little strange that Muhammad Abduh, who had no legal experience whatsoever, should be appointed a judge. However, the main difficulty faced by the National Courts in their early years was a lack of suitably trained personnel. A Khedival Law School had been set up in 1873, but in the absence of adequate funding had failed to develop. By 1880 it employed several language teachers, but only two teachers of law, of whom only one taught the French-style system that was applied in the National Courts. Thus, in the words of one historian of these courts, "a practical *savoir-faire*, not university diplomas, remained the most important qualification" at least until 1890, when examinations for lawyers practicing in the National Courts were introduced. Many established advocates failed these examinations. When this happened, some argued that the previous system had actually been better – judges and lawyers who might not know much law, but who did know the realities and customs of the Egyptian people, were preferable to those who knew the new laws, but were out of touch with realities. A similar argument about the importance of the appropriateness of laws to actual conditions had been made by Muhammad Abduh in *Al-Waqa'i al-misriyya* shortly before the Urabi Revolt.

Muhammad Abduh certainly knew the realities of life in the Egyptian countryside. He had, after all, grown up in a village in the Delta. Three quarters of the disputes that came before him in Banha were between relatives, which somewhat dismayed him, but gave plenty of scope for the application of "practical *savoir-faire*." He is reported to have "applied the law with an independence of judgment in interpretation and a freedom from subservient regard for legal forms that led sometimes to criticisms from the more literally minded." Despite this, his conduct evidently met with approval, as he was transferred first to Zagazig, and then to Cairo where, in 1890, he was appointed to the Court of Appeal. His period of probation in provincial obscurity had lasted only two years.

In Cairo, he applied himself to the study of French, which he had first started to learn as a student in Afghani's circle, and which had presumably improved during his stay in Paris. French was not only the language used by writers such as Guizot, but was also the language that gave access to the literature relating to the laws applied in the National Courts. Muhammad Abduh's approach to the study of French is characteristic. He refused to learn the rules of grammar, and instead used his French teacher to help him read through the works of Alexandre Dumas. A taste for the adventures of d'Artagnan and the three musketeers and for the career of the Count of Monte Cristo was not unusual in Europe at the time, but it was less usual in Egyptian judges. This unorthodox approach worked, as by the end of his life Muhammad Abduh is reported to have spoken "the most perfect French, faultless in its grammar, and almost Parisian in its intonation," and to have read not only Dumas but also Victor Hugo and Molière, not to mention Schiller and Goethe, Kant and Schopenhauer.

## THE AZHAR COUNCIL

The khedive Tawfiq, who evidently saw Muhammad Abduh primarily as a former Urabist rebel, died in 1892, and was succeeded by his son Abbas Hilmi, aged only eighteen. Muhammad Abduh immediately submitted to the new khedive a memorandum on his favorite subject, educational reform, dealing specially with the Azhar. This memorandum was favorably received, and when in 1893 the new khedive set up a commission to propose curricula reform for the Azhar,

Muhammad Abduh was appointed to it. In 1894, the khedive ordered the creation of a six-man Azhar Administrative Council, consisting of the rector of the Azhar, three other senior Azharis, and two government nominees, to replace the old Azhar Council, which had consisted solely of Azharis. One of the government nominees was Muhammad Abduh, and the other was Abd al-Karim Salman, who had formerly worked with Muhammad Abduh on *Al-Waqa'i al-misriyya* and who also came from the old Afghani group. Muhammad Abduh thus returned to the institution where he had started his adult life, which he had not then much enjoyed or appreciated, and with which he had had no significant contact since 1877.

On the subject of the Azhar, Muhammad Abduh and the young khedive were in full agreement. The Azhar mattered because it remained Egypt's main institution of higher education. It was the primary source of Egypt's schoolteachers, preachers, and Sharia Court judges, and also had a significant impact on public opinion. It was, however, a mess: disorganized, plagued by scandal and nepotism, or – in the sarcastic words of the progressive intellectual Uthman Amin – "a species of asylum or retreat for the aged, the indigent and the shiftless." It was also still teaching much the same pre-modern curriculum that it had taught for centuries. Its reform, both in its administration and its curriculum, was thus an essential step in Egypt's development. The khedive, in his own words, wished "to strike a balance between divine matters and humanity," as "no institution has the right to stay outside national life and shirk the duty of national solidarity." The Azhar, as a religious institution, was beyond British control: although the British consul-general did not hesitate to assert his authority over government departments, he followed standard British colonial practice in keeping away from Islam. The khedive, then, could act more or less unilaterally as concerned the Azhar.

Under Muhammad Abduh's leadership, the Administrative Council drafted a law on administration, promulgated in 1896. Together with a salary law, this regularized the composition and powers of the Council, and specified two varieties of degree, both awarded by examination. The lower degree of *ahliyya* required eight years' study and gave access to employment as a primary school teacher or an imam. The higher degree of *alimiyya*, available after a further four years' study, gave access to a teaching post at the Azhar itself and thus to a salary of between 75 to 150 piasters a month. This was considerably lower than the pay received by teachers at the Dar al-Ulum, who earned 400 piasters a month. Presumably in order to lessen hostility to these new measures, existing Azhar teachers could receive up to 300 piasters.

The Council, which met twice a month, established a formal administration, with offices and clerks. It reorganized the Azhar's endowment, increasing annual income from about 400,000 piasters to almost 1,500,000 piasters. It gave the Azhar something of the physical and organizational structure of a modern institution. An official school year was introduced, regular class times were established, and rules were made concerning student attendance. Books were collected from around the Azhar and placed in a new central library, accessible to all. Student accommodation was improved, as was hygiene, partly through bringing in running water and partly by retaining a physician and a pharmacist and ordering regular medical inspections of students.

The Council succeeded in reforming the Azhar's administration, but had less success with the curriculum. It attempted to add to the study of religious topics the study of history, geography, geometry, and Arabic literature, but the central focus of the Azhar's education remained much what it had always been. Although some Azharis favored reform, the majority did not, resenting government interference in their affairs and seeing attempts to add modern subjects as attempts to dilute or destroy the traditional religious curriculum.

Despite this partial failure, the 1890s were a good decade for Muhammad Abduh. He had returned to Egypt, survived two years in the provincial court system, and had been appointed to a position where he could implement some of the reforms that he thought necessary for the development of Egypt. He was rich enough to afford European holidays, for example in 1894 to Evian-les-Bains, the newly fashionable French spa on the shores of Lake Geneva. It was probably during this period that he also took courses in literature and the history of civilization at the University of Geneva. It was also during this period that he published *Risalat al-tawhid*, in 1897.

## APPOINTMENT AS MUFTI

In 1899, the khedive had to appoint a new Mufti of the Egyptian Realm to replace Hassuna al-Nawawi, who he had just dismissed during a dispute about legal reform. The khedive chose Muhammad Abduh.

One of the duties of the Mufti (the others will be discussed below and in the next chapter) was to approve appointments of judges to the Sharia Courts. Although the jurisdiction of the Sharia Courts had been reduced to family law and inheritance, their functioning still gave rise to official concern, and the British adviser at the Ministry of Justice, Malcolm McIlwraith, had proposed appointing two judges from the National Court system (the system in which Muhammad Abduh had sat on the Court of Appeal). The cabinet had agreed, but the Chief Qadi, who headed the Sharia Court system, objected to what he saw as a further attack on the Sharia Courts. Al-Nawawi sided with the Chief Qadi, despite having the reputation of being a reformer – he had been appointed rector of the Azhar at the same time that Muhammad Abduh had been appointed to the Azhar Administrative Council, and had worked for Azhar reforms, despite his growing unpopularity at the Azhar. After the prime minister had failed to persuade al-Nawawi to change his mind, the khedive summoned al-Nawawi and the Chief Qadi, and tried himself. During a stormy meeting, al-Nawawi was dismissed. The Chief Qadi remained in office, since Egypt's peculiar legal position meant that he was appointed not by the khedive but by the Ottoman sultan. These events reversed al-Nawawi's position at the Azhar: instead of being disliked as a reformer doing the business of the British, he became generally respected for his courage and integrity.

The British consul-general, by then ennobled as Lord Cromer, blamed this failure on McIlwraith, who he described as "full of good intentions, but Scotch and unimaginative." An alternative explanation was that the position of Mufti of the Egyptian Realm was not an easy one. Al-Nawawi had lasted only two years in the job, and of Muhammad Abduh's three immediate successors, one would die almost immediately, and the other two would be dismissed, one after nine years and the other after six. The Mufti shared control of the Sharia Courts with the Chief Qadi, not only by way of his role in judicial appointments, but also as one of five judges on the Chief Qadi's Sharia Appeal Court. The Mufti also sat on a number of government bodies, and confirmed death sentences. One potential source of difficulty was that the Mufti, appointed by the khedive of Egypt, had to act together with the Chief Qadi, appointed by the Ottoman sultan. A greater source of difficulty was that the Mufti and the rector of the Azhar had to mediate between the khedive, who appointed them, and the ulema, who they jointly headed, and who were generally hostile to the reforms instituted by the khedive, often at the instigation of the British. The Mufti was also sufficiently senior to be of direct concern to the consul-general, giving him – in effect if not in theory – two masters. In the words of Lord Cromer:

> The Englishman ... could not make the Egyptian horse drink of the waters of civilization, albeit the most limpid streams of social and juridical reform were turned into the trough before him, if the Mufti condemned the act of drinking as impious.

The Mufti's role in social reform resulted from the practice of asking him to declare whether or not a proposed measure was acceptable in Islamic terms, and also from the authority that his office gave him (and the rector of the Azhar) in the public debate. The job of the Mufti, then, was in many ways more political than religious.

Given these difficulties, it is not surprising that Muhammad Abduh hesitated before accepting his appointment. In the end, he did accept it.

## LAW REFORM

As Mufti, Muhammad Abduh's immediate task was the reform of the Sharia Court system, the issue that had led to his predecessor's dismissal. In the true manner of a late nineteenth-century reforming administrator, he set out on a tour of inspection throughout Egypt. At the end of this, he reported that the Sharia Court judges were poorly trained, that the Sharia Courts sat irregularly in dirty and dilapidated buildings, that proceedings were chaotic, and that record-keeping was poor. Most court verdicts were evaded or not enforced, for example when former husbands avoided payments to former wives by spending their money on second wives. Another problem was that the reference books used by Sharia Court judges were not properly organized, in the sense that they lacked indexes, and that rules were mixed in with "controversy, research, and techniques of choosing one rule over another."

Many of these issues resembled those Muhammad Abduh had already encountered on the Azhar Administrative Council, where replacing broken furniture and establishing a regular timetable had also been concerns. In a much-read and somewhat controversial book on Egypt in this period, Timothy Mitchell has borrowed from Michel Foucault to show how Egyptian reformers adopted the contemporary European emphasis on formal order, discipline and cleanliness. Egypt had in previous centuries got on quite happily with informal arrangements, in timetabling as in the structure of books. The reference books used by the Sharia Court judges, for example, certainly lacked indexes, but did follow an organizational scheme of their own, and had never been intended to be used as substitutes for nineteenth-century law codes. The new Egypt, however, demanded new approaches.

The main solutions that Muhammad Abduh proposed were that enforcement of the judgments of the Sharia Courts be made the task of the National Court system, that judges be properly trained, and that the Sharia be codified, i.e. that a modern law code similar to those used in the National Courts replace the existing, uncodified,

Sharia. These proposals differed from those earlier made by McIlwraith and rejected by the Chief Qadi and by Muhammad Abduh's predecessor as Mufti, but they achieved much the same result – and were in a sense more radical, since instead of involving the National Courts in the work of the Sharia Courts as McIlwraith had proposed, they effectively made the judgments of the Sharia Courts subject to the National Courts. Also, McIlwraith had never suggested the codification of the Sharia. A codification had in fact been carried out in 1875, but not enacted; enactment of a codification of the Sharia would not actually happen in Egypt until 1920. Even Muhammad Abduh's less-radical proposal for a school to train Sharia Court judges was not implemented until 1907.

Perhaps in recognition that the codification of the Sharia was unlikely to happen soon, Muhammad Abduh also addressed certain issues in the Sharia itself. Egyptian Sharia Courts were then applying the Hanafi *madhhab*. The term *madhhab*, often translated somewhat confusingly as "school of law," denotes an accumulated body of precedent, an internally consistent interpretation of the Sharia based on a particular exegetical methodology. The Hanafi *madhhab*, named after the eighth-century scholar al-Numan ibn Thabit Abu Hanifa from whom it ultimately derived, was followed by only a minority of the population, but had become the official Ottoman *madhhab*, in which Egypt had followed suit. The Hanafi *madhhab* did not allow judgments *in absentia*, so no judgment could be given when a defendant failed to attend court. This was acknowledged to be a major problem in divorce cases, when a husband could avoid a verdict simply by refusing to attend court. A law of 1897 had attempted to solve this problem by allowing the court to appoint an agent to represent an absent defendant so that proceedings could continue, but Muhammad Abduh reported that this approach was not working and recommended that judges be allowed to apply rules from other *madhhabs*, a controversial procedure known as *talfiq*. He also recommended that judges be encouraged to prefer *maslaha* (in this context, equity) to the letter of the law, an equally controversial proposal. With these proposals, Muhammad Abduh used his early Azhar training to engage with Islam at a level of detail which had not previously interested him, and which would not interest him much in the future. These proposals, then, show an alternative Muhammad Abduh: instead of attacking the entire system of *taqlid* that gave rise to the *madhhabs*, as he had done before, he was proposing technical modifications that had some pedigree within the ulema's world. *Talfiq*, for example, was generally resisted, but had been defended by some ulema.

The pragmatism and moderation suggested by these proposals was not, however, to be the general tone of Muhammad Abduh's period as Mufti.

# 7

# THE MUFTI

Muhammad Abduh, Mufti of the Egyptian Realm, had several jobs. His main task was to provide legal advice in the form of fatwas (*responsa*, non-binding rulings) on questions relating to the issues that came before the Sharia courts: inheritance, endowments, leases, and other aspects of family law. During his six years in office, he issued about one thousand fatwas on these subjects, all of which followed established practice, and so are of little interest. It is possible that he used other ulema to draft these for him, since he produced on average more than three fatwas a week.

As Mufti, Muhammad Abduh also returned to national politics, becoming a member of the Treasury Council, a member of the Council for Endowments, and a member of the Legislative Council. Of these, the council that really mattered was the Council for Endowments, which controlled the assets, mostly real estate, that financed the upkeep of mosques and the activities of the ulema. The property in question was very substantial, and – given its religious nature – beyond direct British control. The Legislative Council, which consisted of fourteen appointed and sixteen elected members, reviewed all proposed legislation, but was purely advisory. Further, it advised the khedive, while real power lay not with the khedive but with the consul-general. It was still of some importance, however, and was the Egyptian equivalent of the Viceregal Legislative Council to which Ahmad Khan had been appointed in India.

The position of Mufti also involved duties at the Azhar, where Muhammad Abduh was already on the Administrative Council.

Originally, there had been not one single Mufti of the Egyptian Realm but four Chief Muftis at the Azhar, one for each of the four *madhhabs*. The role of the Chief Hanafi Mufti had developed over the century into the post to which Muhammad Abduh had been appointed. As a consequence, Muhammad Abduh was also the Azhar's Hanafi Mufti, a post that carried both administrative and teaching duties. His approach to administrative questions was similar to that he took on the Administrative Council, the difference being that he could have a more direct impact, for example in improving admissions standards by the use of an entrance examination for those wishing to study the Hanafi *madhhab*. On some occasions he went further, for example in raising the stipends of students who did well in subjects such as geography and history – though for this he had to use his own private funds.

Initially, Muhammad Abduh tried to teach a full range of courses at the Azhar, but soon gave up – probably because of lack of time – and instead delivered one regular lecture. Over time, these lectures became very popular, and not just with students. They were also attended by members of the public, predominantly from the elite, and even by Christians. Muhammad Abduh would sit in a chair facing the prayer niche, which was illuminated by gaslight, a striking symbol of progress. Next to him was a smaller chair, holding a lantern with four tapers. Thus established, he would deliver his lecture slowly and clearly, with occasional pauses, in a style very different from that generally used by Azhari shaykhs.

The Azhar lectures were one of three ways in which Muhammad Abduh went beyond his required duties to engage in national and international debate. The other two ways were by issuing fatwas on general topics of public interest, and by writing in newspapers, one of which – *Al-Manar* ("The lighthouse") – became very closely identified with him, and carried his messages beyond Egypt to the whole Muslim world. These messages, which would not have surprised anyone who had read *Risalat al-tawhid*, had an extraordinary impact, and in the end changed the nature of Islam – though, as we will see, not necessarily in ways that Muhammad Abduh would have wished.

*Risalat al-tawhid* was written by an exiled Egyptian schoolteacher in Syria. The Azhar lectures, printed in *Al-Manar*, carried with them all the prestige and authority of the world's most famous institution of Islamic learning, and all the prestige of the Mufti of the Egyptian Realm. This might be a position of relatively recent origin, and more of a political than of a religious or a scholarly appointment, but even so it shared in the authority that had attached to the Azhar over the centuries. The basic message did not change much, then, but the medium changed enormously.

## THE AZHAR LECTURES

Muhammad Abduh's lectures at the Azhar were in theory on *tafsir*, exegesis of the Quran, and were presented as *tafsir* in *Al-Manar*. Despite this, rather as *Risalat al-tawhid* is not really about *tawhid* (theology), the Azhar lectures were not really about *tafsir*. They almost totally ignored the established methodology of *tafsir*, since Muhammad Abduh generally took a short Quranic text as his point of departure for a lecture which might be on a general religious topic, or might be on a social topic. For example, Quran 2:170 refers to those who, when asked to follow what God has revealed in Islam, foolishly reply that they prefer to "follow the ways of [their] fathers." A traditional *tafsir* might either discuss some of the pre-Islamic customs that the foolish might have followed, such as "slitting the camel's ear" or explain that the verse was specifically addressed to a group of Jews who had responded to an invitation to become Muslim by saying they preferred to follow the religion of their fathers. In his Azhar lecture on this verse, Muhammad Abduh entirely ignored such concerns, and instead took the verse as an occasion to attack *taqlid*, arguing that it was now not the Jews but the Muslims who were excessively attached to the customs of their fathers. The active researcher who sometimes gets things wrong may well be closer to truth than the sheeplike follower of *taqlid*.

Another example is Muhammad Abduh on the part of Quran 2:165 that runs "Yet there are those who take others besides God *andadan* (as equals), loving them with the love of God." A traditional *tafsir* of this might perhaps comment on the word *andadan*, translated above "as equals," and specify that this means "as equal with God." It might then continue to explain that the verse refers to polytheists in Mecca, who worshiped idols, and who loved them in the sense of "magnifying them and being subservient to them." It might perhaps end by stressing the evils of idol-worship by referring to a *hadith* in which the Prophet Muhammad said that the greatest sin was to appoint a rival to God, while He alone created us. Muhammad Abduh instead took this text as the basis for a discussion of Sufism, explaining that while the early Sufis were great Muslims in terms of their morality and ascetic practice, official persecution forced them to hide their true beliefs behind symbols that subsequent generations took literally, leading later Sufis to hold their shaykhs in excessive reverence, and ultimately to the cult of tombs of saints. Instead of *tafsir*, then, Muhammad Abduh was simply using his text to repeat a view on popular Sufism that he had first expressed in the pages of *Al-Waqa'i al-misriyya* before the Urabi Revolt, and that derived in part from Guizot.

Muhammad Abduh used his Azhar lectures to promote other parts of his reformist agenda as well, for example by arguing against polygamy. Rather than revive the argument of Ahmad Khan that he had once used in *Al-Waqa'i al-misriyya*, he now objected on practical grounds – the inevitable jealousies between different wives, the hostility between children and wives who were not their mothers, and the resulting rows. He also promoted the virtues of hard work, again on practical grounds, avoiding philosophical discussions of the nature of predestination.

Muhammad Abduh also addressed the difficult issue of contradictions between generally accepted Muslim understandings of the universe and the new understandings revealed by natural science. He promoted a "scientific" worldview, arguing for naturalistic, non-miraculous understandings of events related in the Quran.

References to angels, for example, might be to "natural forces." References to "seven heavens" might be to the seven planets (the accepted number in 1900). The famous story of an Abyssinian army that was besieging Mecca being destroyed by stones from on high might refer to the impact of microbes, perhaps of smallpox. Stories such as this were anyhow used in the Quran to give lessons, not to teach history. He even defended Darwin, arguing that natural selection was a device used by God, citing Quran 2:251, which states that "if God had not repelled some men by means of others, the earth would have been corrupted."

## NEWSPAPERS

Muhammad Abduh's first newspaper contributions as Mufti were in *Al-Mu'ayyad* ("The divinely supported"), then recently established but already one of Egypt's leading newspapers, edited by his friend Ali Yusuf, a supporter of the khedive. In 1900, *Al-Mu'ayyad* published a translation of an article by Gabriel Hanotaux, a prolific French historian who had served in the French embassy to Istanbul from 1885 to 1886 and as foreign minister from 1894 to 1898. In an article on French policy toward its North African colonies, Hanotaux had been severely critical of Islam, which he explained in terms of Semitic and Aryan characteristics. He considered that it was the Semitic origins of Islam that led to its requirement for a blind submission to predestination, and that made God remote and so made man helpless. It was Islam, he argued, that was ultimately responsible for Arab decadence. This was a similar argument to that made in 1883 by Renan, who also blamed Arab backwardness on Islam and on the Arab race.

Muhammad Abduh responded to Hanotaux in *Al-Mu'ayyad*, as Afghani had once responded to Renan in the *Journal des débats*. Like Afghani, Muhammad Abduh argued against explaining Arab decadence in terms of race and Islam by providing another explanation. Unlike Afghani, he did not write of the hostility of religion in general to reason, but of the negative impact of Sufism. Also unlike Afghani, he addressed the Semitic/Aryan question directly. It was not Islam that had led to decadence, but Sufism, and Sufism was actually of Aryan origin (in this Muhammad Abduh was following theories then generally accepted in Europe, though nowadays mostly rejected). Europe had in fact benefited from contact with Semitic Arab civilization during the middle ages. And predestination was not the problem: the Islamic understanding of predestination was actually more complex than the Christian. Muhammad Abduh's response seems to have been generally well received in Cairo as a defense of Islam, though presumably it was less well appreciated by any Sufis who read it, and by Muslims whose understanding of predestination was closer to classical Sunni norms than was Muhammad Abduh's.

From 1902, however, Muhammad Abduh wrote not in *Al-Mu'ayyad* but in *Al-Manar*, a newspaper that was to become closely associated with him and would be very important in spreading his message. *Al-Manar* had been founded in 1898 by a Syrian immigrant, Rashid Rida, who had studied in Beirut under Husayn al-Jisr, the director of the Sultaniyya, where Muhammad Abduh had himself taught. Rida later explained his move to Egypt in terms of a desire to work with Muhammad Abduh, by whose articles in *Al-Urwa al-wuthqa* he had been inspired as a young man. While Rida had no doubt been inspired by *Al-Urwa al-wuthqa*, an additional explanation is that he – like so many other Syrian journalists – found a more congenial atmosphere in Egypt than in Syria, where journalism was stifled under the autocratic rule of Sultan Abd al-Hamid. Rida had at first attempted to start a newspaper in his native Tripoli, but his application had been refused on the grounds that there was already one newspaper in Tripoli, and that if there were two, the burden on the censor would be too great. When he left Syria for Egypt, he traveled with a friend who also had journalistic ambitions, Farah Antun, a Christian. In Egypt, Antun started *Al-Jami'a al-uthmaniyya* ("The Ottoman Community"), and Rida started *Al-Manar*.

The declared purposes of *Al-Manar* were to promote social, religious, and economic reform, to encourage tolerance, unity, education, and progress in arts and sciences, and also "to prove the suitability of Islam as a religious system under present conditions, and the practicality of the divine Sharia as an instrument of government." Initially, *Al-Manar* was a weekly publication of 8 pages with a print run of 1,500 copies, but this was soon reduced to 1,000 copies, published monthly. In 1902, *Al-Manar* had only about 350 subscribers.

The occasion for Muhammad Abduh first writing in *Al-Manar*, and thus for a substantial increase in *Al-Manar*'s circulation, was an article on Ibn Rushd published by Antun in *Al-Jami'a al-uthmaniyya*, in which Antun argued in favor of science and philosophy. Muslim suspicion of Ibn Rushd in particular and of science and philosophy in general, he alleged, derived from a refusal to conceive of God as a first cause who, once the task of creation had been accomplished, withdrew and allowed natural law to reign. This was a particularly Muslim problem: the teaching of Ibn Rushd had survived in Europe, not the Islamic world. Rida encouraged Muhammad Abduh to respond to Antun in *Al-Manar*, which he did, asserting that in fact Islam did not see God as directly responsible for everything that happens, and that Christianity had not been as tolerant as Antun suggested. Further, Islam was actually more rational than Christianity, as well as more tolerant. The exchange between Antun and Muhammad Abduh continued for several issues, doing wonders for the circulation of both newspapers. After its completion, both sides published their versions – Antun as *Ibn Rushd wa falsafatuh* ("Ibn Rushd and his philosophy"), and Muhammad Abduh as *Islam wa al-nasraniyya* ("Islam and Christianity").

From this point, *Al-Manar* proceeded to publish Muhammad Abduh's lectures, a series which finally became famous as the *Tafsir al-Manar* ("*Al-Manar*'s Quranic Exegesis"). This is now probably Muhammad Abduh's best-known work after *Risalat al-tawhid*. It is not known quite what Muhammad Abduh thought of *Al-Manar* or even of Rida, but he must have approved in general, despite the fact that he never promoted the "divine Sharia as an instrument of government." He often allowed Rida to attribute Rida's own writings to him.

*Al-Manar*'s circulation gradually grew until it was being read across the Muslim world, where Arabic was still the common language of communication for intellectuals as well as ulema – intellectuals who were not ulema, in fact, were only then beginning to emerge as a distinct category. In Malaya, for example, the distinction was made between the *kaum muda* or "new generation" and the established ulema, who came to be known by extension as the *kaum tua* or "old generation". For the *kaum muda*, *Al-Manar* was of great significance. Sometimes they took ideas from it, as when they proposed the use of *talfiq*, the application of rules from various *madhhabs*, especially controversial in Malaya, where only one *madhhab* was followed. More important, though, was the way in which *Al-Manar*'s mere existence justified and legitimized their struggle against the local ulema establishment, almost irrespective of *Al-Manar*'s content. First, *Al-Manar* showed that the *kaum muda* were not alone, and allowed them to present themselves as the local representatives of a general movement of reform and renewal. They might be few, but the movement as a whole was large. Second, *Al-Manar* came from Cairo, the home of the Azhar, and was in Arabic, the language of Islam. Even though Malaya had had its own ulema for centuries, an Arab provenance was still seen as guaranteeing an authenticity, and conferring a prestige, that could not be found locally.

Small groups such as the Malay *kaum muda* existed everywhere, the result of socio-economic change and exposure to Western education and values, and they all drew inspiration from *Al-Manar*. Such groups sometimes addressed distinctively local issues (such as Hindu influences on Malay Islam), but also addressed general issues that were broadly similar, whether in Russian Central Asia or in Cairo, since their origins were ultimately the same: European penetration of the Muslim world, in politics, economics, thought, and natural science.

Another reason for *Al-Manar*'s great influence was that it had no rival. There was no other significant "Islamic" publication, as the ulema everywhere generally avoided the new medium of print journalism. This left the field open to their rivals. The ulema's apparent negligence is explicable. A similar quandary had faced the Catholic Church in Europe after the Reformation: to use the new medium of printing and enter into the public debate was to accept defeat, since one of the issues at stake was precisely whether there should be a public debate, or whether the knowledge and authority of the established guardians of religious truth rendered any such debate inappropriate and unnecessary. The Azhar, for example, did not launch a publication of its own until 1931.

## EDUCATION

In 1904, Muhammad Abduh lamented to the French travel writer Amédée de Guerville that Egypt trained lawyers, physicians, and engineers, but provided nothing of any value in the humanities, social sciences, or economics. "You will not find an inquiring man, a thinker, a philosopher or scholar in the educated classes," he told her. "You will not find one man of broad intellect, of aspiring soul, or noble feeling." This was something of an exaggeration, as even Muhammad Abduh would really have had to admit, if only as concerned some of his own associates, with whom he continued to work, in a private capacity, for the improvement of education in Egypt. Chief among these was his old friend Saad Zaghlul, now a lawyer in the National Courts with a degree in law from Paris, and also with good connections among the Egyptian elite, first through his relations with Princess Nazli Fadil, to whom he had been introduced by Muhammad Abduh, and then through his marriage to Safiyya Fahmi, daughter of Prime Minister Mustafa Fahmi.

Zaghlul shared Muhammad Abduh's conviction that Egypt badly needed a good institution of higher education, not just professional training, and both men finally abandoned earlier hopes that the Azhar might be reformed into a real university. Zaghlul, Muhammad Abduh, and some others therefore decided to work for the foundation of an entirely new institution. Muhammad Abduh's main part in this was in convincing a rich landowner, Ahmad Pasha al-Minshawi, to donate a plot of land to be used for the purpose. The land in question was not, however, considered to be in a suitable place. Muhammad Abduh also founded, in 1900, a Society for the Revival of Arabic Books, which published a number of new editions of Arabic classics.

Zaghlul and Muhammad Abduh were also concerned with primary education, and for this purpose founded, in 1892, a Muslim Benevolent Society, which was to some extent modeled on the Syrian charity of the same name. Also on the board of this society, of which Muhammad Abduh became president in 1900, were Hasan Pasha Asim, later Grand Chamberlain to the khedive, two more lawyers (Ahmad Lutfi and his brother Omar), and an employee of the State Domains Administration, Muhammad Talaat Harb. Many of these were later to become famous.

The main objective of the Benevolent Society was to set up schools where the poorer classes might have a basic education on the modern European model, though without foreign languages, to prepare them for life as craftsmen or in similar humble occupations. That the children in these schools should not come to despise such occupations was one of their objectives. By 1905, the Benevolent Society had established seven such schools, teaching 770 children. Although this is not a large number, it is significant compared to the government's own school program, which was also tiny – at the time when the Benevolent Society was established, there were only nine government-run primary schools, teaching 2,460 children. More Muslim children were taught by Christian missionaries, who in 1893 already taught 7,130 children in 108 schools. By 1906, the United Presbyterian Church of Philadelphia alone had 171 schools in Egypt, teaching over 15,000 children, including over 3,000 Muslim children. The Benevolent Society, then, should be seen as doing what it could do with the limited resources that were available.

Muhammad Abduh's new enthusiasm at this point in his life was the work on education of Herbert Spencer, which he translated from French into Arabic. While on holiday in Europe in 1903, he went to Brighton to visit Spencer, then eighty-three years old and with only months left to live, taking with him as interpreter (since Spencer evidently did not speak French) none other than Wilfrid Blunt.

Spencer is less well known today than he was in 1903, but at the time his works sold in astonishing numbers. One aphorism of Spencer may well have appealed to Muhammad Abduh: "To the superstitions that pass under the name of religion, science is antagonistic; but not to the essential religion which these superstitions merely hide." Spencer's book on education argues against learning by rote without understanding, and also against the punishment of children, partly on utilitarian grounds, and partly because the faults of children derive, at least in part, from the failings of their parents. It argues for valuing the physical education of girls as much as that of boys, and not forcing children to eat what they do not want to eat. The views that Muhammad Abduh evidently so much appreciated, although written in 1861, would command general agreement in liberal educational circles today. It is not known to what extent Muhammad Abduh was able to see them implemented in the schools run by the Benevolent Society.

# THE FATWAS

Although the majority of Muhammad Abduh's official fatwas were neither remarkable nor controversial, the fatwas that he issued on what would today be called consumer finance were both remarkable and controversial. Even more controversial was one particular fatwa issued not in his official capacity as Mufti of the Egyptian Realm, but in the pages of *Al-Manar*: the so-called "Transvaal Fatwa."

## FINANCIAL FATWAS

Many of the reforms carried out in Egypt during Muhammad Abduh's life aimed at fostering economic development by introducing a modern physical, administrative, legal, and financial infrastructure. They included the introduction of a modern commercial code of law which allowed for the creation of limited-liability companies, sometimes quoted on an Egyptian stock exchange, and for the issue of Egyptian government debt, both in Egypt and on foreign exchanges. None of these devices were known to classic understandings of the Sharia, which would have condemned most if not all of them, but this did not give rise to significant problems, since they were regulated not by the Sharia but by the new law codes administered by the Mixed Courts and the National Courts. Some controversy arose, however, when it was realized that the Council for Endowments was following the normal practice of other government departments and placing funds on deposit at the National Bank.

Interest was earned on these deposits, and classic understandings of the Sharia held that taking interest was forbidden, that money that arose as interest was thus impure, and that anything paid for with that money was also impure. To apply impure money to government purposes was one thing; to apply impure money to religious purposes was another.

What was generally more controversial was consumer finance: interest-bearing deposit accounts, and property and life insurance. These were clearly legal under the new codes of national law, but were generally regarded as forbidden by the Sharia. While this had no effect from a purely legal point of view, it still discouraged the use of these devices. This concerned the Egyptian government most in the case of post office savings accounts, which were not just potentially useful for the general population, but were also a source of government finance, in Egypt as in other countries.

Muhammad Abduh issued several fatwas on consumer finance, starting in 1901 with a fatwa that legitimized property insurance. This had previously been considered forbidden by the Sharia on the dual grounds that a contract of insurance is a contract based on an uncertain future event, and that insurance is in substance a gambling transaction – that the insured is, in effect, betting that his or her house will burn down. To the modern Western mind, of course, the reverse is true – insurance is designed to reduce risk, and failing to insure one's house is gambling that it will not burn down. Property insurance thus provides a neat illustration of the conflict between a strict understanding of the Sharia and modern analyses and practices. It was to be expected that Muhammad Abduh would rule in favor of the modern.

In 1903, Muhammad Abduh issued two more fatwas on consumer finance, one dealing with interest, and one dealing with life insurance. In one of his Azhar lectures, he argued that "a part of what the ulema class as *riba* [interest] brings no injustice; in fact, there is sometimes benefit in it for he who gives and he who receives." The argument made here is utilitarian rather than based on exegesis, much as his argument against polygamy was. The text of his 1903 fatwa on post office savings accounts no longer exists, but it seems that instead of referring to utility, he argued for the legitimacy of payments to depositors that were calculated as a profit-share under the classic Sharia device of the *mudaraba* partnership agreement. Alternatively, he may have argued for the legitimacy of a "dividend" of up to two-and-a-half percent, distinguishing this from usurious interest. Whatever, the khedive appointed a commission of ulema to look into the question, later saying that he did so to prevent Muhammad Abduh issuing a fatwa that would have allowed all forms of interest.

The fatwa on life insurance, also issued in 1903, took a similar approach, interpreting life insurance in terms of *mudaraba* and so allowing it. In the conception of the fatwa, the insured gives money to the insurance company, which then after a specified period returns not only the money but a share of the profits it has made with that money. However, if the insured dies, the money is collected instead by his heirs. This is a description of what is technically known as a "with-profits endowment policy," and is more or less accurate, so far as it goes. What Muhammad Abduh omitted was the two elements that would raise problems under the Sharia: the pure insurance element in the arrangement, which means that the sum collected by the insured's heirs after an early and unexpected death is greater than the premiums that have been paid, and the origin of the profits, which commonly includes interest from bonds as well as from other forms of investment. While Muhammad Abduh may have omitted discussion of the interest problem because he had an incomplete knowledge of the investment practices of life insurance companies, he must have known that the sum that would be collected in the event of an early death was greater than the premiums then paid. At least one omission, then, was almost certainly intentional.

## THE TRANSVAAL FATWA

Perhaps Muhammad Abduh's most famous fatwa, however, was the "Transvaal fatwa," also issued in 1903, and so called because it was given in answer to questions raised by Muslims in the Transvaal, the former Boer republic in South Africa that had just been conquered by Britain. That Muslims in the Transvaal should address a Mufti in faraway Egypt was an indication of how far Muhammad Abduh's fame had already spread, for though the Muslim community in the Transvaal was small, the Muslim community in Cape Town and Durban was substantial and long established, and a lot closer than Cairo.

Three questions were asked in the Transvaal fatwa. Two related to disputes in the South African Muslim community, which was split between the followers of the Shafi'i and Hanafi *madhhabs*, the former of whom were the oldest established group, and the latter of whom consisted mostly of more recent arrivals from India. The Hanafi *madhhab* had been promoted in South Africa by a Kurdish member of the ulema despatched by the Ottoman government. He had also encouraged Muslim men to wear the fez, which the Ottoman government had recently approved as an alternative to the hat, which the Ottoman ulema deemed unsuitable for Muslims since the brim of the hat prevented the forehead from touching the ground during the prostration that was part of the ritual prayer. One of the questions, then, was whether a Muslim might wear a hat. Despite the fact that Egyptian Muslims did not wear hats either, and that the fez was worn in Egypt as it was in the Ottoman Empire, Muhammad Abduh replied in the affirmative, so long as the wearing of a hat did not "indicate an intention of copying the Europeans in their religion, but has a practical purpose." This, of course, was not what was generally thought to be the issue.

Another question was whether a Shafi'i Muslim might follow a Hanafi imam in prayer. The reason for this question was that the split between the Shafi'i and Hanafi communities in South Africa had given rise to separate mosques for Shafi'is and Hanafis, a practice that some Muslims in the Transvaal evidently wished to challenge. Again, Muhammad Abduh replied in the affirmative, on this occasion following the general view of the Egyptian and Ottoman ulema.

The third question related not to a dispute but to what must have been a practical problem for the small number of Muslims in the Transvaal: whether a Muslim might eat meat from animals slaughtered by Christians. The generally accepted answer to this question was that Muslims might only eat meat killed properly according to the Sharia, notably when the name of God had been said at the slaughtering of the animal concerned. Presumably, however, there were then no Muslim butchers in many parts of the Transvaal (though there were certainly Muslim butchers elsewhere in South Africa).

Muhammad Abduh had already encountered this problem since he had lived in Paris, where there were probably then no Muslim butchers either, but it is not known what he had done under these circumstances. He had written in *Risalat al-tawhid* that Islam, as the third and complete revelation, encouraged amity between peoples by allowing Muslims to share the food of followers of the earlier revelations. This was not as radical as it might seem, however. The ulema would have agreed, since the Quran specifically states that the "food" of the Jews and Christians is allowed to Muslims – but most of the ulema would then have added that "food" did not include meat. The meat eaten by Christians included pork, for example, which everyone agreed was not allowed to Muslims. There was not, however, total unanimity on other meats, and in his fatwa Muhammad Abduh held that "food" did include meat, referring to the opinion of a respected but minor Andalusian scholar of the eleventh century, Abu Bakr Muhammad Ibn al-Arabi al-Maliki.

## MUHAMMAD ABDUH'S METHODOLOGY

In recent years, there has been much discussion among scholars, both Western and Muslim, about what Muhammad Abduh's methodology was. Methodology is more important in Islam than in religions such as Christianity, because the ulema have, since antiquity, attempted to the best of their ability to extract the rules of the Sharia from the texts left by the original revelation of Islam. The relationship between the Quran and the *hadith*, for example, has been an important issue. Greater emphasis on one or the other leads to different conclusions on many questions. Another issue has been which *hadith* to accept and which to reject – there is a great mass of *hadith* material, and it has always been accepted that some of it is apocryphal, and should be discarded as unreliable. The question has been over where and how to draw the line. Once again, different conclusions result from different methodological approaches. Muhammad Abduh is not recorded as having said much on questions of methodology, which is one reason why there has since been so much discussion over what his methodology was.

Muhammad Abduh could well have written at length on technical methodology if he had wanted to. He was familiar with the issues from his Azhar training, and sometimes used classic and later-medieval Islamic scholarship to support his arguments, as when he referred to Abu Bakr Muhammad Ibn al-Arabi al-Maliki. However, as has been said, he did not write at any length on methodology, and in general – as in his Azhar lectures – spent little or no time examining the basis on which a conclusion was based. It seems, then, that he was more concerned with the conclusion than with the methodology used to reach it. In the classic Sunni conception, a conclusion should be reached by the application of the proper methodology to the sources through which the original revelation is known. If – for example – the conclusion is that insurance is forbidden, then insurance is forbidden, and that is that. Muhammad Abduh seems to have taken the opposite approach – that if insurance is a good thing, then it is a good thing, and questions of methodology do not really matter. In *Risalat al-tawhid*, he wrote critically of the effects of theological disputation, which he evidently regarded as unnecessary. The source of his objections to polygamy, to Sufism, and to lack of hard work is not a particular exegetic methodology, then. It is his reading on topical issues, his reflections on these, and his experience over the years.

Despite this, Muhammad Abduh did implicitly promote a new variety of exegesis: that of defying *taqlid*, both in the technical legal sense of refusing to follow a single *madhhab* and in the more general sense of refusing to be bound by tradition, by precedent and custom, of reading the Quran anew, ignoring prior interpretations.

# MUHAMMAD ABDUH'S INTENTIONS

Muhammad Abduh's attempt to legitimize practices from wearing hats to using life insurance were part of a general attempt to remove Islamic prohibitions against modern European usages. He is said, for example, to have argued against the classic prohibition on the making of images on the grounds that the danger of images being worshiped as idols was now long past. He is even said to have issued a fatwa allowing Muslims to pray with their shoes on, a practice that he adopted – at least on occasion – himself.

By the 1890s, Muhammad Abduh was clearly an enthusiast of Europe. On his unusual habit of taking European holidays, he wrote:

> I go to Europe so often only to renew my hope of changing the conditions of the Muslims for the better by reforming the religion that they have corrupted, and to spur them to a knowledge of their own affairs and a control over these without going to extremes. And these hopes would grow feeble in my soul when I came back to my own country because of all the wrongdoing I came in contact with, the grave difficulties I encountered, the evils I saw because of the Muslims' disregard for their own advantage, their hostility towards themselves, their great eagerness to strengthen the grip of their oppressors on them, and their fondness for unthinking servitude to them. But when I returned to Europe, and stayed there a month or two, my hope would come back to me, and it would seem easy to attain what I had thought impossible.

This, rather like Muhammad Abduh's comment to Amédée de Guerville on the absence of original thinkers in Egypt, suggests a measure of depression. The cause of this – the "great difficulties" that Muhammad Abduh encountered – will be discussed in the following chapter. The enthusiasm for Europe, however, is also clear – but it was an enthusiasm within limits.

In 1903, Muhammad Abduh traveled to Algiers. He had initially wanted to go with his friend Ali Yusuf, editor of *Al-Mu'ayyad*, with whom he had visited the Ottoman capital in 1901, but he went alone, as his friend did not receive the necessary permission from the French authorities. Algiers had been under French control since 1830, and was in 1903 perhaps the most European of all Arab cities, known for its "*évolués*" – "developed" Algerians who were effectively French in language, culture, and even legal status. Muhammad Abduh stayed with one such *évolué*, a rich and cosmopolitan Algerian whose house was known for its parties and concerts. On this occasion, predictably, he argued in private conversation for reform of Islamic education, and of Islam itself, to adapt to modern conditions. Less predictably, he argued against the abandonment of Algerian identity, since he thought it unlikely that Algerians would ever be accepted as fully French, whatever they did. This argument is consistent with a view reported by Lord Cromer, that Muhammad Abduh considered "the Europeanized Egyptian" "a bad copy of the original" – a view that Cromer himself seems to have shared. For all his appreciation of Europe, then, Muhammad Abduh remained convinced that Europe was a model, not a destination. He may have wanted to legitimize a range of modern European practices, but he did not wish Egypt, or Algeria, to become Europe.

Muhammad Abduh's views on identity are less clear than his views on some other issues, but may have been important for his work, and may also explain part of his own relationship with Islam. The connection between religion and identity in the Arab world, and hence between religion and nationalism, is complicated. The broadest definitions of the Egyptian nation, such as those promoted in *Al-Tijara* before the Urabi Revolt, relegate religion to a secondary position in order to include Egyptian Christians (and, once, Jews). Older, religiously based conceptions of the community persist, however, and in practice Islam remains central to the national identity of Muslim Egyptians, whatever the theory. In a certain sense, a patriotic Egyptian has to be Muslim. Muhammad Abduh's promotion of an Islam that was adapted to modern conditions and was acceptable to modern patriotic Egyptians, then, was not just protecting Islam, but also protecting the Egyptian identity.

# 9

## ADVERSITY

"If I have a portion of true knowledge," said Muhammad Abduh, "I got it through ten years of sweeping the dirt of the Azhar from my brain, and to this day it is not as clean as I would like." The response of the Azhari Shaykh Bukhayri, to whom Muhammad Abduh addressed this comment, is not recorded. The response to Muhammad Abduh and his message of the Azhar in general, though, is known. It was generally hostile, and grew more hostile as time passed.

The ulema of the Azhar had grown used to attack ever since Mehmet Ali had first acted to reduce their power shortly after he became ruler of Egypt. Over the nineteenth century, they had seen the government, acting under the excuse of reform, seize their personal investments, then the endowments that supported their jobs, and generally remove as much as possible of their independence, while promoting rival institutions. They had seen the government of Egypt change from an Ottoman-style regime that, if not especially pious, was at least respectful of the forms of Islam, to a government evidently dedicated to transforming Egypt into a copy of Christian Europe under the khedive Ismail, and then finally to a government that acted under direct British control. And now the attack against them was being led by one of their own, an Azhari like themselves, Muhammad Abduh. First Muhammad Abduh appeared as the representative of the government on an Administrative Council that they had never asked for, more interested in the promotion of secular European learning than in the promotion of the study of Islam. Then they saw him appointed Mufti of the Egyptian Realm, despite his lack of any appropriate scholarly record, a position that he then used to attack Islam — or, at least, what they understood as Islam. Instead he promoted a version of Islam that seemed to owe more to Europe than to the Quran or the *hadith*.

Opposition to Muhammad Abduh at the Azhar was intense from the beginning. The other shaykhs, according to a student of the time, "used to constantly criticize the Shaykh [Muhammad Abduh] in our presence and represent him as being dangerous for religion." As a result, the former student went on, "I used to flee from encountering the professor, for the sake of my religion, and to flee from listening to his lessons, even though he was a friend of my father."

*Risalat al-tawhid* had been directed toward the type of modern Muslim who might be tempted to reject Islam as an old *thobe*, and his message as Mufti was much the same as his message when teaching at the Sultaniyya. It was not really directed at the sort of Muslim who still wore a *thobe*, and was in no way embarrassed by Islam — the sort of Muslim to be found in villages such as that in which Muhammad Abduh had grown up. One student who was not afraid to listen to Muhammad Abduh at the Azhar was Taha Husayn, later one of Egypt's leading intellectuals and writers. After one year at the Azhar, he returned home for a visit, and with the naivety of youth explained "true" Islam to anyone who would listen — which ended up being quite a lot of people. The general conclusion, in Taha Husyan's own, later words, was:

> He has been up to Cairo to sit at the feet of Shaykh Muhammad Abduh and imbibe his dangerous and abominable opinions; and now he has come back to lead his townsfolk into error and perdition.

This was to be expected, and Muhammad Abduh could probably have handled opposition in such quarters with the support of the khedive and of educated public opinion. Both of these he lost, however, until his single remaining supporter of significance was Lord Cromer, a type of support that ultimately rendered his position impossible.

## OPPOSITION IN THE PRESS

Most of the "quality" Egyptian press supported Muhammad Abduh. *Al-Mu'ayyad* was edited by a friend, and *Al-Ahram* was as progressive as Muhammad Abduh himself was – as well as being owned by Christians, who were not especially concerned about what was and was not "true" Islam. *Al-Muqattam* and *Al-Watan* were also broadly in favor.

Two newspapers, however, became early critics. One was *Al-Zahir* ("Illumination"), edited by Muhammad al-Sharbatli, an established opponent of Muhammad Abduh. The other was *Himarat Munyati* ("Donkey of my desire"). As the title suggests, this was an unusual newspaper – especially in Arabic, a language in which the word "donkey" is somewhat rude. *Himarat Munyati* was a relatively short-lived weekly, started in 1899 and lasting only until 1904, which published entertaining stories and political news in colloquial rather than formal Arabic, and which stood outside both the political and journalistic establishments. Its editor, the son of an army officer, was pointedly not admitted to the Egyptian Press Association. It was in some ways a forerunner of the later "yellow" or "tabloid" press, and in some ways the successor the *Abu Naddara*. While *Abu Naddara* and Muhammad Abduh had been on the same side in 1877, *Himarat Munyati* and Muhammad Abduh were on different sides in 1901.

*Himarat Munyati* first started attacking Muhammad Abduh in January 1901, with an article criticizing him for allowing the funds under the control of the Council for Endowments to be invested in the National Bank and so to earn interest. So-called reform, it added, was really just serving the interests of foreigners, at the expense of the Egyptian people. In July it attacked Muhammad Abduh for his views on predestination – the views which he had advanced in 1900 in his refutation of Hanotaux, and which had also been expressed on other occasions. The classic understanding of predestination was not incorrect or the cause of Islamic decay, as Muhammad Abduh suggested. It was the correct teaching of Islam. If Muhammad Abduh believed otherwise, as he evidently did, the explanation was that he was a heretic, influenced by European philosophies of free will. In October, *Himarat Munyati* asked why Muhammad Abduh was more interested in visiting European spas and going to Geneva than in going to Mecca on the hajj pilgrimage. "Someone who attached so little importance to his religion" was not fit to be Mufti of the Egyptian Realm, especially when he was helping the British to increase school fees in order to keep Muslims out of Quran schools, while giving extra money to Azhar students for doing well in geography and arithmetic, but not for doing well in Islamic subjects.

On March 1, 1902 *Himarat Munyati*'s front page carried a photograph that was, to European eyes, unremarkable. It was a group photograph taken, probably, at a garden party. In the front row sits a mustachioed European gentleman between two elegantly dressed ladies, one of whom is reading a book. In the back row stands another gentleman, also between two elegantly dressed ladies, with one of whom he is conversing happily. What rendered the photograph unusual was that the gentleman in the back row was dressed in the robes of an Azhar shaykh. A shaykh, said *Himarat Munyati*, had evidently become a *khawaga* – the colloquial and somewhat pejorative term for a Christian foreigner.

*Himarat Munyati* did not name the shaykh, but the shaykh was very visibly Muhammad Abduh. And although the fashion in which his female companions were dressed was entirely respectable in European terms of 1902, as was the manner in which Muhammad Abduh was conversing with one of the ladies, neither the dress nor the physical proximity between him and the lady were in the least respectable in Egyptian terms. The scene was later described by a supporter of Muhammad Abduh (who may or may not have seen the actual photograph, which he described as "fraudulent") as "an obscene picture" of the Mufti "in an obscene position" with a dancer – dancers being, in Egypt at that time, much the same thing as prostitutes.

*Himarat Munyati* was not a mass-circulation newspaper. However, the rector of the Azhar, with whom Muhammad Abduh shared the pinnacle of official Islam in Egypt, demanded the prosecution of the editor of *Himarat Munyati* in order to preserve the reputation of the Mufti. A prosecution was started, putting Muhammad Abduh in an impossible position – he could either confirm that the photograph was genuine, in which case he would have to resign from his official positions in disgrace, or he could stay silent, in which case he would be party to the punishment of an innocent man, even if the innocent man was an opponent of his.

Muhammad Abduh chose to stay silent. The editor of *Himarat Munyati* was sentenced to three months' imprisonment. The publicity attending the trial ensured that anyone who had not already seen the photograph at least heard about it. Muhammad Abduh became the object of ridicule, as is suggested by a cartoon of the time which shows a shaykh embracing a scantily dressed European lady. A small dog paws at the shaykh's robes – dogs are considered impure by classic Islam, and so any Arab caricature stereotyping Westerners as both alien and somewhat disgusting will probably include a dog. The caption of the cartoon reads, simply, "His Excellency Muhammad Abduh, Mufti of the Egyptian Realm."

That Muhammad Abduh thus became the object of ridicule was not simply the fault of the editor of *Himarat Munyati*. The publication of the photograph was said to have been approved in advance by the rector of the Azhar, the very man who then made the photograph famous by calling for a prosecution to defend Muhammad Abduh's honor. And the ultimate source of the photograph was said to have been Prince Muhammad Ali, the brother of the khedive.

## DETERIORATING RELATIONS WITH THE KHEDIVE

Muhammad Abduh and the khedive seem to have remained on good terms until 1902, even though Muhammad Abduh had angered the khedive in 1901 by lunching with Ahmad Urabi. In 1902, two disputes occurred, one over the fate of a British spy and the other over a Greek island.

The British spy was Leon Fahmi who, having worked for the British in Istanbul, retired to Egypt. The Ottoman authorities knew of his presence there, and requested his extradition. The khedive wished to oblige the Ottoman government, but the British wished to protect their former employee. The khedive therefore summoned Fahmi to his palace, where Fahmi was arrested. Cromer, alerted that Fahmi had failed to return from his appointment at the palace, went himself to see the khedive, who swore on his honor that Fahmi was not in the palace – which was quite true, as Fahmi was in fact being held in a nearby house. Cromer, who was not convinced, extracted Fahmi from the khedive's custody, and had him sent under protection to safety in France. This episode left Cromer feeling satisfied, and presumably left the khedive feeling humiliated. That Muhammad Abduh had opposed sending Fahmi to Istanbul meant that he had effectively sided with the British against his sovereign in a matter of some importance.

The second dispute concerned the Aegean island of Thasos, which was of importance because of its strategic location and its gold mines. This island had originally been given to Mehmet Ali by the then Ottoman sultan, and was a significant possession of the khedive. After a rising by the Greek inhabitants of Thasos against the khedive's attempts to increase taxes, Ottoman troops occupied the island. The British proposed to replace the Ottoman troops with their own, which the khedive did not wish to happen. Muhammad Abduh proposed to allow a British occupation.

After these two incidents, which affected the khedive personally, it is understandable that the khedive might come to the conclusion that Muhammad Abduh was more loyal to the British than to himself. The khedive later described Muhammad Abduh as "of remarkable intelligence, but pusillanimous character. He was devoted to England. I tried in vain to tear him away from the lure of Qasr al-Dubara [Cromer's residence]."

What is less clear is why Muhammad Abduh took positions, on issues that were not central to his activities, that would inevitably make an enemy of the khedive. There are two possible explanations.

One is that Muhammad Abduh was indeed siding with Cromer, with whom he was on excellent terms. Cromer, who remembered Muhammad Abduh as "a somewhat dreamy and unpractical but, nevertheless, genuine Egyptian patriot," seems to have liked and even respected him, and described Muhammad Abduh in his memoirs as "my friend." The khedive thought that Cromer paid more attention to the views of Muhammad Abduh than to those of any other Egyptian. The other possible explanation is that Muhammad Abduh was simply continuing the stance he had taken earlier in his life, when he had stood against an earlier khedive, Ismail. Perhaps his views on the need to limit khedival power had not changed as much as might have been thought on the basis of his quiet participation in the machinery of the Egyptian government since his return to Egypt from Beirut. This explanation is perhaps more likely since – whatever the khedive may have thought – Muhammad Abduh was not an uncritical supporter of the British. Although he sided with Cromer on some issues, he disagreed on others.

A further clash between Muhammad Abduh and the khedive in 1902 did concern an issue that was central to his activities as Mufti: the annual hajj pilgrimage to Mecca. For Muslims, to perform the hajj once in a lifetime is not only a religious duty for those in a position to do it, but is also often the high point in an individual's life. To die on the pilgrimage ensures admission to heaven. For the British, in contrast, the annual hajj was of concern largely because, as the occasion for the close meeting of pilgrims from several parts of the world, it served as a central node for the spread of infectious diseases. To prevent the spread of disease to Egypt, and then perhaps via the Suez canal to Europe, an obligatory quarantine station for returning pilgrims had been established in the Sinai desert in 1877. In early 1902, however, a cholera epidemic broke out in the Philippines that ultimately killed some 200,000 people there. As a precaution, the British wanted the khedival government to ban Egyptian participation in that year's hajj. Muhammad Abduh supported the British proposal. The khedive, the rector of the Azhar, and the prime minister all opposed the proposal. One result was that Egyptians participated in the hajj as usual, and brought cholera back to Egypt: 34,600 people died. Another result was that Muhammad Abduh had publicly stood with the British and with medical precautions against Islam and a united front of Egypt's other religious and political leaders.

After 1902, hostility between Muhammad Abduh and the khedive grew worse. During 1903, as we have seen, the khedive interfered in Muhammad Abduh's activities as Mufti by establishing a commission of ulema to investigate the question of interest paid on post office savings accounts. According to the khedive, this was to thwart Muhammad Abduh's own planned fatwa on the subject, a fatwa of which Cromer had seen the draft before the khedive. Muhammad Abduh, in turn, interfered with the khedive's affairs by using his position on the Council for Endowments to prevent a sale to the khedive, at a price considerably below its market value, of some land in Giza that belonged to the Council. In Muhammad Abduh's eyes, this would have been an attempt by the khedive to steal from the Council. In the khedive's eyes, Muhammad Abduh would have been preventing him from drawing funds for his "national project" from one of the few remaining sources that were not under British control.

At this point, Muhammad Abduh issued his Transvaal fatwa.

## REACTIONS TO THE TRANSVAAL FATWA

*Himarat Munyati*, of course, seized upon the Transvaal fatwa as a further stick with which to beat the Mufti. On this occasion, so did many others, including even *Al-Liwa*, the newspaper of Mustafa Kamil, with whom Muhammad Abduh had until then been on good terms.

The response which caused the problem was, of course, that which allowed Muslims to eat meat killed by Christians. The attack in the more serious press was launched by *Al-Zahir* in December 1903, with the headline "How can that be declared lawful which God has declared unlawful?" *Al-Zahir* followed up in January 1904 with an appeal to the ulema of the world to reject the fatwa, and a demand for the dismissal of Muhammad Abduh from his post as Mufti, on the technical grounds that in relying on a Maliki scholar (Abu Bakr Muhammad Ibn al-Arabi) he was not following the Hanafi *madhhab*, which as Mufti he was legally obliged to do.

Muhammad Abduh was defended by the progressive press – *Al-Muqattam*, *Al-Ahram* and *Al-Watan* – as well (of course) as by *Al-Manar*, which had published the fatwa in the first place. Muhammad Abduh responded to *Al-Zahir* in *Al-Manar* sarcastically, remarking that while Christians do not consecrate their meat to Jesus, some Muslims do consecrate theirs to Ahmad al-Badawi, the great Sufi saint.

Placed in the context of his deteriorating relations with the Azhar, the khedive, and sections of the Egyptian public, Muhammad Abduh's decision to publish the Transvaal fatwa at this point requires explanation. He can hardly have supposed that his permission to eat meat killed by Christians would pass without reaction. A prudent person might have thought that he needed to consolidate his position rather than endanger it further, and he had been behaving in a generally prudent fashion since he broke with Afghani, except – perhaps – by antagonizing the khedive over questions of fugitive spies and Aegean islands, when he might have compromised without imperiling his main projects. Perhaps he thought he could consolidate the support of progressives; or perhaps he thought that the opposition of his enemies was so great that nothing would make any difference. Or perhaps he no longer really cared.

## RESIGNATION

In January 1904, the breach between Muhammad Abduh and the khedive became more public. The khedive asked that a vacant professorship at the Azhar be given to a scholar who was serving as Mufti to the khedival cabinet. The Azhar Administrative Council gave the professorship to someone else. When asked by the khedive why this had happened, Muhammad Abduh replied – in public – that the Council was bound by the law, not by the orally expressed wishes of the khedive. Unsurprisingly, the khedive was – according to his private secretary – furious. Not only had Muhammad Abduh defied him in public, but he also seemed to be attempting to end the khedive's influence in one of the few areas that the British had so far not interfered with.

Muhammad Abduh carried on for another year. During 1904 he chaired a commission looking into the reform of the education of Sharia Court judges, continuing the task of reforming the Sharia Courts that had been the occasion of his appointment as Mufti in the first place. He also drafted a bill on the organization of mosques, which was passed into law during the same year, setting out minimum qualifications for various posts, from the imam to the muezzin who gave the call to prayer. Towards the end of 1904, however, the khedive delivered a public speech in which he denounced Muhammad Abduh personally. At this point, even the small following Muhammad Abduh had among students at the Azhar deserted him. Hostile comment in the press became ever more frequent.

On January 14, 1905, the khedive asked Lord Cromer to agree to the removal of Muhammad Abduh from his position as Mufti. Cromer refused, although Muhammad Abduh expressed his willingness to resign. On March 19, however, Muhammad Abduh resigned from the Azhar Administrative Council. He also resigned from the Council for Endowments.

Muhammad Abduh had evidently decided that his days as Mufti were over. His determination to leave government service was known, and a supporter had given him some land on which to start a school. He may even have been thinking of emigrating: in 1905 he visited the Sudan, where he had for some time been advising the legal secretary of the British-run Sudan Government on the Sudanese Sharia Court system. While this may have been routine business, Muhammad Abduh may have been looking for a new job.

# DEATH

Muhammad Abduh, however, fell ill. On his way to Europe for treatment, his condition worsened, and he stopped in Alexandria at the house of Muhammad Bey Rasim, in the Ramleh district. There, at 5 p.m. on July 11, 1905, he died of cancer of the kidney, aged fifty-six.

He did not, however, die in disgrace. A special train was arranged to take his body to Cairo, stopping on the way several times for crowds to pay their last respects. In Cairo he was given a state funeral, with a cortege from the rail station to the Azhar that included officials, diplomats, army and police officers, Azhar students, and "a vast concourse of people from all classes and religious faiths." He was buried in the Mujawirin cemetery. At the commemoration which in Egypt traditionally marks forty days after a death, "a great crowd again gathered."

One of the many who attended the funeral was Ahmad Shafiq Pasha, a lawyer and prominent courtier. When he returned from the funeral, the khedive addressed him as follows:

> But don't you realize that this man was the enemy of God, the enemy of the Prophet, the enemy of religion, the enemy of the doctors of the faith [ulema], the enemy of the Muslims, and the enemy of himself?

# THE ENEMY OF GOD?

Although it had been said, wrote Lord Cromer, that "an upper-class Moslem must be 'a fanatic or a concealed infidel,'" he thought Muhammad Abduh was neither. "I suspect that my friend Abdu, although he would have resented the appellation being applied to him, was in reality an Agnostic," wrote Cromer, after Muhammad Abduh's death.

Cromer was certainly right in saying that Muhammad Abduh was not a "fanatic," if by that word he meant a Muslim who was unwilling to contemplate any alternative to generally accepted understandings of Islam. Muhammad Abduh's message was, in that sense of the word "fanatic," directed against fanaticism. Cromer was also right in saying that Muhammad Abduh was not a concealed infidel, but probably not right in seeing him as agnostic. We have only caught occasional glimpses of Muhammad Abduh's private religious views, but these glimpses do not really suggest agnosticism. One of the most intriguing glimpses in later years is of Muhammad Abduh performing the ritual prayer with his shoes on, a practice that he (as we have seen) is said to have issued a fatwa to defend. Nearly all Muslims, of any variety, were and are fully agreed that shoes should be removed before the prayer. Quite why Muhammad Abduh disagreed is not known, but performing the prayer with shoes on is convincing evidence that Muhammad Abduh was neither a "concealed infidel" nor an agnostic. An agnostic or an infidel might perform the ritual prayer for the sake of appearances, but no one who was interested in appearances would pray with his shoes on.

It is interesting that Muhammad Abduh remained an active Freemason even as Mufti – though he evidently denied this to Rashid Rida, who explained in *Al-Manar* that while Muhammad Abduh had once been a Freemason, he had since "cleaned himself internally from Masonry." Muhammad Abduh's name, however, appears in a return for 1901 held in the archives of the French Grand Orient in Paris, along with that of Butrus Ghali Pasha, the prime minister. It is possible that Cromer belonged to the same lodge. Saad Zaghlul also remained a Freemason, though it is not known whether he was in the same lodge as Muhammad Abduh. Muhammad Abduh's earlier participation in Freemasonry can be explained in terms of his participation in Afghani's revolutionary conspiracy, but his political views as Mufti were very different. His continuing participation in Freemasonry might be explained in terms of the useful contacts it provided. It might also be explained, however, in terms of Muhammad Abduh being a sincere believer in the Masonic ideal of working to better the lot of humanity.

# 10

# THE AFTERMATH

Despite Muhammad Abduh's death, he continued to have an impact on Egyptian life, as did many of the individuals with whom he was associated, and whom he had to some extent inspired. Some of Muhammad Abduh's projects were completed by these associates, even though some of his other achievements were undone.

## PUBLIC LIFE

After the death of Muhammad Abduh, Lord Cromer redirected his support to Muhammad Abduh's closest friend and colleague, Saad Zaghlul. In 1906, at Cromer's insistence, the khedive appointed Zaghlul minister of public instruction. One of Zaghlul's first acts was to establish the school for Sharia Court judges that Muhammad Abduh's commission had proposed in 1904, and in 1908 the Egyptian University for which he and Muhammad Abduh had worked was also opened. It had proved impossible to reform the Azhar to produce properly trained judges for the Sharia Courts, and it had proved equally impossible to reform it to produce "an inquiring man, a thinker, a philosopher." The school for Sharia Court judges produced the one, however, and the Egyptian University (later renamed Cairo University) produced the other, at least until it was transformed into a different, and far from rigorous, mass university during the Nasser period. In two important respects, then, what Muhammad Abduh had been working for was achieved soon after his early death.

Zaghlul was not the only associate of Muhammad Abduh to move from administration into politics, with some encouragement from Cromer. In 1906 a group including several members of the Benevolent Society established a company to publish an anti-khedival and liberal newspaper, *Al-Jarida*, which appeared in 1907 under the editorship of Ahmad Lutfi. Shortly after *Al-Jarida* started publication, however, Cromer resigned as consul-general and returned to England, mostly for health reasons. He was replaced by Sir Eldon Gorst, who quickly reversed a major aspect of Cromer's policy by seeking a rapprochement with the khedive. When in late 1907 the group around *Al-Jarida* founded a political party, the Umma Party, with Ahmad Lutfi as secretary, its opposition to the khedive led to a different relationship with the British. Although not exactly hostile to the British, the Umma party did not enjoy the same cooperative relationship with them that Muhammad Abduh and then Zaghlul had once enjoyed with Cromer.

Zaghlul, however, became minister of justice in 1910, and then under the very different conditions that existed after the First World War became Egypt's leading nationalist politician. His arrest by the British in 1919 sparked riots that are sometimes described as a revolution, and that certainly led Britain to give up direct control over Egypt. Following his release, Zaghlul founded what became one of Egypt's main political parties, the Wafd Party. As leader of this party, he served as prime minister, and won three elections. If, during the interwar period, he never quite achieved Egypt's full independence, he without doubt did more towards that than any other Egyptian. Ahmad Lutfi initially joined Zaghlul's Wafd Party, but then retired from politics. He served as rector of the Egyptian University for many years, and was briefly minister of education from 1928 to 1929.

Among others of Muhammad Abduh's associates, Omar Lutfi might have continued to similar prominence, but died in 1911. Talaat Harb became the leading proponent of economic nationalism, establishing a private Bank of Egypt that grew into a massive holding company. Subsidiaries of Talaat Harb's bank established Egypt's first film studios and, in 1937, the airline that is now called Egyptair.

Talaat Harb, Saad Zaghlul, and Ahmad Lutfi played major roles in producing what was seen by many intellectuals at the time as an Egyptian renaissance – which was precisely what, in the last resort, Muhammad Abduh had always worked for. Although this renaissance had begun to run out of steam by the 1950s, when it was replaced by the problematic "Arab Socialist" regime of President Nasser, for some decades Egyptian public and intellectual life changed significantly, in much the direction that Muhammad Abduh wanted.

The achievements of Talaat Harb, Saad Zaghlul, and Ahmad Lutfi were of a variety that Muhammad Abduh himself could hardly have envisaged, given that circumstances between the world wars were so different from those he had known. British weakness lay as much beyond his imagination as film studios and airlines. Muhammad Abduh was only one influence on the development of these men, who also drew directly on the progressive European thought that Muhammad Abduh had drawn on. Muhammad Abduh, however, still deserves some credit for what his younger associates achieved later in their lives, and so for the emergence of a newly independent, modern and – for a time – self-confident Egyptian nation state. His reputation as an Egyptian patriot is deserved, then.

## ISLAM

If Egyptian public and intellectual life changed in the direction that Muhammad Abduh wanted, religious life at first changed less, and then changed in other directions. In the short term, many of Muhammad Abduh's most notable positions concerning Islam were reversed, and in the long term, new understandings of Islam became widespread that were very much against the spirit of Muhammad Abduh's own understanding.

Muhammad Abduh's successor as Mufti, Muhammad Bakhit, immediately published a condemnation of property insurance as forbidden on the classic grounds that it was in effect a form of gambling. The same conclusion was reached by another Mufti, Abd al-Rahman

Kuraha, in 1925. When, in 1926, the Sharia Court of Appeals came to consider a case involving a with-profits endowment life insurance policy of the sort that Muhammad Abduh had approved in 1903, it refused to order a payment to the appellant, on the grounds that the entire contract was illegal and so unenforceable. Consumer finance remains little used in Egypt even today – though there are reasons for this that have nothing to do with Islam, and derive ultimately from the socialist system that was set up by President Nasser. In other parts of the world, an "Islamic finance" industry has developed that in 2007 managed assets worth some $500 billion. Like Muhammad Abduh, this industry aims to make modern financial instruments available to observant Muslims. It does so, however, by modifying the form of the financial instrument and leaving intact the generally accepted interpretations of the Sharia. Muhammad Abduh tried to leave the form of the financial instrument intact, and to modify interpretations of the Sharia. The alternative approach has worked better.

Fatwas on other topics were not reversed, but were generally ignored. A small minority of Muslims do follow Muhammad Abduh's fatwa on meat slaughtered by Christians, but the vast majority do not. The "Halal butcher" has become a central feature in the life of the Muslim diaspora in Europe. Although Muslims today sometimes wear hats and only very rarely wear the fez, this is a result of the abolition of the fez by modernizing states that saw it not as a symbol of Islam but as a symbol of the old monarchical regimes.

Two basic ideas that Muhammad Abduh had promoted did become generally accepted. One was that Islam should not be an obstacle to progress. Progress, of course, can be understood in many different ways. The other was the rejection of *taqlid*. Most urban Egyptians today do not think of themselves as following a *madhhab*, for example, but rather as following Islam. This is not equally true everywhere in the Muslim world, especially in countries where there has only ever been one *madhhab*, but in general *taqlid* is no longer an issue. Some current legislation in Egypt and other Muslim countries, mostly on questions such as divorce and inheritance, is based on the Sharia. Recent legislation in these areas has generally followed an approach similar to that used by Muhammad Abduh, based on *talfiq* and *maslaha* rather than *taqlid*, and Muhammad Abduh deserves credit for this.

The more general demise of the *madhhabs* also owes something to Muhammad Abduh's influence. Many later writers and thinkers promoted their own visions of a non-*madhhab* Islam, from Rashid Rida to Hasan al-Banna, the founder of the Muslim Brothers, a very successful mass movement that has had an extraordinary impact on the entire Muslim world. In Rida's case, the general idea of a non-*madhhab* Islam can be traced to Muhammad Abduh, though the understanding of Islam was different, as we will see below. Al-Banna likewise owed the general idea of a non-*madhhab* Islam indirectly to Muhammad Abduh, though again the understanding of Islam was different.

The demise of the *madhhabs* results also from the success of a very different religious reform movement, however, started by Muhammad ibn Abd al-Wahhab in the Arabian peninsula in the late eighteenth century. This movement was of little importance in Muhammad Abduh's time, when it appeared to have been defeated by military action in the days of Mehmet Ali, but in the mid-1920s its proponents captured the holy cities of Mecca and Medina and established the Kingdom of Saudi Arabia, a state which has since promoted its understanding of Islam very successfully. Muhammad ibn Abd al-Wahhab's reform movement thus received a type of backing that Muhammad Abduh's did not.

Muhammad ibn Abd al-Wahhab, like Muhammad Abduh, denied the validity of the *madhhabs*. He called for an unmediated reading of the original texts from which they were derived, the Quran and the *hadith*. His objection to *taqlid* was not that it prevented the exercise of reason – which was, in the end, Muhammad Abduh's objection – but rather that *taqlid* contained *too much* human reasoning, and so was something other than the original divine revelation. The Egyptian ulema of the time rejected this view partly because the followers of Ibn Abd al-Wahhab seemed to them to be simply replacing one interpretation with another. In contemporary Western terms, they were certainly doing this, since every act of reading is necessarily an act of interpretation. This may not be obviously true when the text being read is a newspaper, but it is clearly true when the text being read is as complex as the Quran and *hadith* are, especially when taken together. The Egyptian ulema also objected, of course, because the interpretation that the followers of Ibn Abd al-Wahhab were rejecting was that which they themselves guarded and promoted

Although extreme hostility to the *madhhabs* later vanished from the teachings of the official ulema of Saudi Arabia, the original condemnation of *taqlid* remained alive in other circles, and has since spread from Saudi Arabia to many other parts of the Muslim world. In the end, the demise of the *madhhabs* owes as much or more to Muhammad ibn Abd al-Wahhab as to Muhammad Abduh.

What has replaced the *madhhabs* is not, in general, the rationalist, liberal Islam that Muhammad Abduh promoted. During the twentieth century, it was versions of the interpretation of Islam espoused by activists such as Hasan al-Banna, and then versions of the Saudi interpretation of Islam, that became ever more influential. Hasan al-Banna's interpretation was far from nineteenth-century liberalism, and the Saudi interpretation was in no way rationalist or liberal.

Muhammad Abduh's understanding of Islam, however, was not entirely lost. It remains alive in two, somewhat different, circles. One of these is the descendants of the Egyptian class where Muhammad Abduh was appreciated in his lifetime. This class lost its position as Egypt's elite during the Nasser period, but has not vanished. There are still Egyptian Muslims in Cairo who, like Muhammad Abduh, have read and appreciated the classics of modern Western thought, who speak French and English as well as Arabic, and who love Egypt and would never want to be anything but Egyptian, even if they are frequently exasperated and even dismayed by the behavior their fellow Egyptians. These Egyptians, like Muhammad Abduh, are more concerned with conclusions than with methodology, and may worry less about the details of Islam than about broad principles – which generally include such virtues as self-help and honesty.

The other circle in which Muhammad Abduh's understanding remains alive consists of later "modernist" intellectuals who, like him, want to promote an Islam that is appropriate for the modern world – which they see globally, not locally. These intellectuals generally pay more attention to methodology than Muhammad Abduh did, but even so are working in his spirit. Rather as Muhammad Abduh tried to show that there was no contradiction between Islam and science, the Sudanese intellectual Abdullahi Ahmed An-Na'im, for example, has tried to show that there is no contradiction between Islam and the Universal Declaration of Human Rights. Others, such as the Egyptian Nasr Abu Zayd and the Algerian Mohammed Arkoun, have attempted to reconcile Islam with contemporary Western humanism. Such intellectuals, however, have limited influence, and reactions against them in the Muslim world have often been extremely hostile. All those mentioned above moved to Europe or to the United States.

That Muhammad Abduh's understanding of Islam has become that of a small minority is not just because of the popularity of alternative understandings, notably versions of the Saudi understanding. It is also because the liberal rationalism that inspired Muhammad Abduh has been on the defensive in the Arab world since the late 1930s, rather as it was in Europe during the period of fascism and communism, and in some ways for similar reasons.

## VIEWS ON MUHAMMAD ABDUH

Little attention was paid to Muhammad Abduh in Egypt for some twenty years after his death, but Rashid Rida carried on publication of *Al-Manar* until his own death in 1935, himself completing the *tafsir* that had started with Muhammad Abduh's Azhar lectures. Requests for fatwas that once might have been sent to Muhammad Abduh were now sent to Rida, for example by some Muslims in Indonesia who in 1907 asked whether a Muslim might drink wine, beer, or any of their ingredients. It might have been interesting to see how Muhammad Abduh would have handled such a question – but Rida was more predictable.

Over the years, Rida became increasingly identified with Muhammad Abduh. Rida promoted the memory of Muhammad Abduh, and the memory of Muhammad Abduh promoted Rida. Without formal religious or scholarly credentials, and as something of an outsider in Egypt, Rida was in need of legitimization, and this was provided by his link with Muhammad Abduh, which he emphasized, presenting himself as Muhammad Abduh's closest disciple – despite the fact that he had known him only the last eight years of his life, and that if any one person was obviously close to Muhammad Abduh throughout his whole life, it was not Rida but Saad Zaghlul. One reason that Rida was able to do this was that no one else was much interested in claiming the position of Muhammad Abduh's successor. Muhammad Abduh's former associates moved on into new roles which did not need religious legitimization. Zaghlul's activities, for example, were legitimization enough in themselves. Also, by the time that Rida published his *Tarikh al-ustadh al-imam al-shaykh Muhammad Abduh* ("History of Professor the Imam Shaykh Muhammad Abduh") in 1931, most of Muhammad Abduh's closest associates were dead, and so could not comment either on Rida's portrayal of Muhammad Abduh or on Rida's portrayal of himself.

Rida differed from Muhammad Abduh and his former associates both politically and intellectually. Politically, he was committed to the anti-imperialist nationalism that became more and more popular after the First World War, in Syria as well as Egypt – a position very different from Muhammad Abduh's cooperative relationship with Lord Cromer, or even the purely Egyptian nationalism of Saad Zaghlul in the interwar period, but close to the radical pan-Islamist position that Muhammad Abduh had once promoted from Paris in *Al-Urwa al-wuthqa*. Intellectually, Rida never shared Muhammad Abduh's enthusiasm for European civilization, or for European ideas. He was inspired not by Guizot or Spencer, or even by Persian philosophers, but by classic Islamic scholars such as Ibn Taymiyya, the often hard line Hanbalite whose work was used extensively by the followers of Ibn Abd al-Wahab in Arabia.

Rida shared Muhammad Abduh's objections to *taqlid* and the *madhhabs*, but not his emphasis on the conclusions. His continuation of Muhammad Abduh's *tafsir* in *Al-Manar* is much closer to classical *tafsir*, both in its conclusions and in its methods. Rida, for example, quotes from the *hadith* in the normal way, which Muhammad Abduh rarely did. Rida objected to Sufism not so much because of the role it seemed to have played in a historical scheme, but because the activities of the Sufis were *bida*, without sanction in the earliest texts.

The views of Muhammad Abduh that Rida promoted were, naturally, those closest to his own. The same was true of the picture of Muhammad Abduh that emerged from Rida's *Tarikh*. Muhammad Abduh's conviction that the abandonment of true Islam was the cause of Muslim decline remained, but the nature of that true Islam changed. Rather than a proponent of reason, Muhammad Abduh became a restorer of Islamic orthodoxy, an opponent of *bida* – and an enthusiast of Ibn Taymiyya. His more unusual views were either ignored or actively deleted from the editions of his works that Rida prepared after the original trustees of these texts – people like Saad Zaghlul – had become too occupied by other matters to complete their task. Rida's edition of *Risalat al-tawhid* differs in significant ways from Muhammad Abduh's original. Certain important details of Muhammad Abduh's life also vanished – the admiration for Guizot, the Freemasonry, and the excellent relations with Cromer.

When interest in Muhammad Abduh revived some twenty-five years after his death, partly because reform of the Azhar was again on the agenda, two pictures of him were available. One was that provided by Rida. The other was that promoted in books such as a short biography by Mustafa Abd al-Raziq, published in 1925. Mustafa Abd al-Raziq had been one of the few Azhar students to appreciate Muhammad Abduh's lectures there, and he had later followed a career similar to those of Muhammad Abduh's younger associates, who were of course themselves older than he was. He taught at the school for Sharia Court judges and at the Egyptian University before going to France in 1909, where he obtained a PhD. In 1925, he was professor of philosophy at the Egyptian University. As might be expected, his biography of Muhammad Abduh stressed rationalism. As a slightly later biographer in the same spirit, Uthman Amin, wrote, what mattered was Muhammad Abduh's "attempt to reform religion, his summons to free thought from the bonds of tradition." This interpretation was presumably also in the mind of the distinguished Egyptian painter Muhammad Naji when, in the 1930s, he included Muhammad Abduh in a painting entitled "The School of Alexandria" along with Alexander the Great, Saint Catherine of Alexandria (also known as Saint Catherine of the Wheel), Archimedes, the modern Greek poet Constantine Cavafy (who lived and died in Alexandria), and the modern Arabic novelist Taha Husayn, perhaps the greatest symbol of the Egyptian renaissance – and also an admirer of Muhammad Abduh.

Both Rida's picture and the alternative picture agreed that Muhammad Abduh was an Egyptian patriot and a reformer, which was certainly true. The pictures disagreed, however, about the thrust of the reforms – toward reason or toward orthodoxy – and about the nature of the man himself – modern intellectual or religious scholar.

As time passed, the Rida view of Muhammad Abduh became the dominant one, enshrined in Egyptian school history lessons and in popular memory. Muhammad Abduh's learning was stressed, and became more and more Islamic in its nature. His piety was respected, and his patriotism admired. As classic texts similar to those that Muhammad Abduh had once studied with Afghani became better known in the Sunni world, it became ever easier to find classic Islamic precedents for many of his views – precedents which may indeed have affected his reading of his nineteenth-century European thought, even if the historical analysis used in this book does not see them as his most important sources. As more and more emphasis came to be placed on these classic Islamic precedents, Muhammad Abduh's other sources were increasingly ignored.

As the details were almost entirely forgotten, Muhammad Abduh receded into the past. While the twenty-fifth anniversary of his death had been celebrated by a series of articles in *Al-Ahram*, then Egypt's leading newspaper, and the fortieth anniversary was marked by a speech by King Faruq (the title of khedive was replaced by the title of king in 1922), the hundredth anniversary in 2005 was marked only by a small conference jointly arranged between the Egyptian National Library and a French academic institute, the CEDEJ. The speakers included the Mufti and the rector of the Azhar, but even so, the anniversary passed almost unnoticed.

In addition to the pictures presented by Rida and by men such as Mustafa Abd al-Raziq and Uthman Amin, a third picture emerged in the West, assisted by the enthusiasm of certain Western scholars, notably Charles Adams, the American Christian author of the only full biography of Muhammad Abduh to appear in a European language during the twentieth century (in 1933). For Adams, Muhammad Abduh's achievement was to bridge the gap between conservative Muslims and progressive intellectuals who had received European educations, a view that both underestimated the conservative resistance and overestimated Muhammad Abduh's success. Muhammad Abduh's impact was also overestimated by Kenneth Cragg, an Anglican bishop and expert on Islam who co-translated Rida's version of *Risalat al-tawhid* into English, and who thought that Muhammad Abduh's "teachings, personality, and influence constituted the most decisive single factor in the twentieth-century development of Arab Muslim thought and renewal."

Although Malcolm Kerr argued in 1966 that "Abduh's historical role was simply to fling open the doors and expose a musty tradition to fresh currents. His intention may have been more specific, but the effect was not," Muhammad Abduh remained a crucial figure in the Western conception of the development of Islam, understood increasingly in the terms that mixed Cragg's judgment with that which had become current in the Arab world, derived from Rida. It thus came as something of a shock when, in 1966, Elie Kedourie published *Afghani and 'Abduh: An Essay on Religious Unbelief and Political Activism in Modern Islam*. In this book, Kedourie used newly discovered documents that Afghani had left behind when he was expelled from Persia to challenge very effectively the general view of Afghani, and used the connection with Afghani to question the general view of Muhammad Abduh. Like many revisionist accounts, this went somewhat too far. Kedourie's conclusion "that by the end of the 1870s the erstwhile mystic, outwardly a divine, was secretly a free thinker" cannot really be sustained. A more balanced account was later produced by a Tunisian scholar working in France, Mohamed Haddad, but this is available only in French, and has so far had little impact.

The final twist in the understanding of Muhammad Abduh came when the term "Salafi" became increasingly popular to describe a movement that had arisen in Saudi Arabia during the 1960s and that insisted on the original teachings of Ibn Abd al-Wahhab rather than the more moderate version of them which had become official in Saudi Arabia. The identification of Osama bin Laden with the Saudi Salafi movement led to some occasional confusion among Western students and sometimes journalists, who sometimes tried to connect Muhammad Abduh with al-Qaeda. It also led to complaints by neo-Wahhabi Salafis that Muhammad Abduh had not been a "real" Salafi, "real" Salafism being defined as their own.

## CONCLUSION

To someone who had met Muhammad Abduh in Paris with Afghani, the idea that this young Egyptian revolutionary might one day be remembered as Mufti of the Egyptian Realm would have seemed most unlikely. A future such as that which awaited Muhammad Abduh's friend Saad Zaghlul, as first political prisoner of the British and then nationalist leader, would have seemed altogether more probable. There was, however, an underlying logic that united all phases of Muhammad Abduh's career. As a young man, he worked through journalism and politics for the improvement of the conditions under which his fellow Egyptians lived. As Mufti, he worked – still partly through journalism – for the same end.

The attempts at transforming the Egyptian system of government in which Muhammad Abduh participated in his youth failed, ultimately because of reasons beyond the control of anyone in Egypt: the seemingly inexorable expansion of European power produced British control of Egypt and so for a time put an end to autonomous political development there. Immediately after the British occupation of Egypt, Muhammad Abduh turned his energies to the promotion of something not so very different from the global revolution that al-Qaeda was to attempt at the start of the twenty-first century. Muhammad Abduh, however, relatively quickly replaced a policy of confrontation with one of cooperation and moderate change. As a moderate committed to cooperation, he became Mufti of the Egyptian Realm.

Muhammad Abduh was a most unlikely Mufti. He was an intellectual in the modern Western sense, though equipped to deal with religious questions by his early training at the Azhar. His intellectual world was very different from that of the ulema, as a result of his earlier life, his travels abroad, and above all as a result of his reading of the period's leading social and political theorists. His approach to many of the problems that came before him as Mufti drew on this unusual intellectual world rather than on classic theories of methodology, and indeed it was part of his approach to focus more on the conclusion than on the technical methodology used to reach it.

This approach made Muhammad Abduh both famous and controversial. For those who shared his intellectual world he was a hero, a progressive figure very different from the far-from-progressive majority of the ulema. He succeeded in showing that Islam did not need to be an old *thobe* in which it was embarrassing to appear, and that it was possible to be modern, Egyptian, patriotic, progressive, and Muslim at the same time. Islam was thus safeguarded, and so was the Egyptian identity. For many of those who did not share his intellectual world, however, he was a collaborator who was barely even Muslim. This was unjust: if he did in some sense follow a policy of collaboration, he was never a collaborator for selfish reasons, but because he saw no better way of achieving what had always been his fundamental objective: the improvement of conditions in Egypt. If his understanding of Islam was unusual, he seems to have remained a believer. He always remained a patriotic Egyptian.

Muhammad Abduh's liberal modernism was very much of its period, a period which was in many ways hospitable to it. Muhammad Abduh became the most prominent and influential representative of the liberal modernist trend within Islam because, as Mufti of the Egyptian Realm, he had more authority than any other representative of that trend, because of *Al-Manar*, and because of what an admirer called his "superabundant and unabated energy," which allowed him to be prominent in so many areas at the same time – writing, lecturing, delivering fatwas, active on the Legislative Council and the Council for Endowments, active in the Benevolent Association, and still with time to visit his many friends. But as circumstances changed, which they did quickly over the twenty years after his death, the space for rationalist liberal modernism contracted. Relations between the Muslim world and the West changed as European power weakened and Egyptian and Arab nationalism gained strength. Egyptian politics changed as social and economic developments produced first the student demonstration and then the Nasserite state. Guizot was forgotten as communism and fascism rose and finally fell in Europe, and as the Islamic Revolution transformed Iran and paved the way for a new "clash of civilizations."

Muhammad Abduh neither revived true Islam nor proposed an alternative to it. He attempted to address the problems of Egypt through Islam, creating in the process a certain synthesis of Islam and of modern thought, thought that was modern in terms of the nineteenth century, not of the twentieth or twenty-first. The emphasis was more on the modern thought than on the Islam, and the synthesis did not prove to be a lasting one, partly for this reason, partly because Muhammad Abduh was more of a pragmatist than a theorist, and ultimately because his work reflected the circumstances of his age, an age that was soon to pass.

# GLOSSARY

*bida* innovation in religion, an undesirable practice not sanctioned by the original revelation of Islam.

**Council for Endowments** the Egyptian government body responsible for the administration of the land and other assets that had been given over the centuries for the upkeep of mosques and to support the activities of the ulema.

**fatwa** a *responsum* or non-binding ruling on a difficult issue relating to the interpretation of the Sharia.

*hadith* reports of the words and actions of the Prophet Muhammad, regarded by classic Islamic jurisprudence as equal in importance with the Quran as a source of the Sharia.

**hajj** the "pilgrimage" ceremonies performed once a year in Mecca around the ancient temple believed by Muslims to have been built by Abraham.

**imam** generally, the leader of ritual prayer in a mosque. Sometimes used as a title for a great religious scholar or leader.

**jihad** warfare against non-Muslims.

**khedive** title given to the hereditary ruler of Egypt from Ismail to the First World War, being a compromise between "king" and "prince."

*madhhab* an established body of exegetical methodology and of generally accepted conclusions; one of four or five internally consistent interpretations of the Sharia; a denomination.

*maslaha* expediency, that which is in the general interest. In a legal context, equity.

**Mufti** religious scholar or official charged with the giving of fatwas.

**pasha** Ottoman title equivalent to the British "lord" held by senior officials and ministers, generals, or grandees.

**piaster** unit of currency in the Ottoman Empire and khedival Egypt. In Egypt, after 1885, 1 piaster was worth about 0.075 grams of gold.

**Quran** the text of the revelation believed by Muslims to have been given by God to the Prophet Muhammad.

*salaf* the first generations of Muslims immediately following the death of the Prophet Muhammad, whose understanding and practice of Islam were exemplary; a group used as a point of reference by several entirely separate movements of religious reform or renewal.

**Salafi** member of any one of a number of distinct movements, all of which claimed or claim to be returning to the pure Islam of the *salaf*, but which have little else in common.

**Sharia** the right way of living for a Muslim, as derived from the Quran and *hadith*; hence the detailed rules indicating proper Islamic practice, in life and worship; hence law derived from Islam.

**shaykh** title of respect, given especially to Azhar graduates or the leaders of Sufi orders.

**Shi'a** the smaller of the two mains sections into which the Muslim community split in its early centuries, following its own distinct understanding of the Sharia. Now found mostly in Iran (formerly Persia), Iraq, and Lebanon.

**Sunni** the larger of the two mains sections into which the Muslim community split in its early centuries, following its own distinct understanding of the Sharia. Now found in most parts of the Muslim world that are not Shi'i.

**Sufi** a member of a *tariqa* or order, within Sunni or Shi'i Islam, promoting optional devotional religious practice, often of a mystic variety; associated in some areas with popular religion.

*tafsir* exegesis of the Quran; commentary exploring the full sense and meaning of the original text.

*talfiq* "piecing together" a conclusion from more than one *madhhab*.

*thobe* gown originally worn by men in the Arab world, used in the late nineteenth century mostly by the poor.
*turba* small tablet of baked clay used by the Shi'a when praying, especially when praying on a carpet or mat.
**ulema** scholars, especially those devoted to the study, explication, and application of Islam.

# FURTHER READING

## CHAPTER 1

The two most useful sources for Muhammad Abduh's life are Charles C. Adams, *Islam and Modernism in Egypt: A Study of the Modern Reform Movement Inaugurated by Muhammad 'Abduh* (London: Oxford University Press, 1933), and Uthman Amin, *Muhammad Abduh* (Cairo: Dar ihya al-kutub al-arabiyya, 1944), trans. Charles Wendell (Washington, DC: American Council of Learned Societies, 1953).

The most useful source for Afghani's life is Nikki Keddie, *Sayyid Jamal al-Din "al-Afghani": A Political Biography* (Berkeley: University of California Press, 1972).

For late pre-modern Islamic education, see Dale F. Eickelman, "The Art of Memory: Islamic Education and its Social Reproduction," *Comparative Studies in Society and History* 20 (1978), pp. 485–516.

For *Risalat al-waridat*, see Oliver Scharbrodt, "The Salafiyya and Sufism: Muhammad 'Abduh and his *Risalat al-waridat* (Treatise on mystical inspirations)," *Bulletin of the School of Oriental and African Studies* 70 (2007), pp. 89–115.

## CHAPTER 2

For the events and personalities of these years, see F. Robert Hunter, *Egypt under the Khedives, 1805–1879: From Household Government to Modern Bureaucracy* (Pittsburgh: University of Pittsburgh Press, 1984), and Arthur Goldschmidt, *Biographical Dictionary of Modern Egypt* (Boulder: Lynne Rienner, 2000).

Accessible primary sources include Wilfrid Scawen Blunt, *Secret History of the English Occupation of Egypt: Being a Personal Narrative of Events* (1907; new edition, New York: H. Fertig, 1967), and his *Gordon at Khartoum: Being a Personal Narrative of Events in Continuation of a Secret History of the*

*English Occupation of Egypt* (London: Swift, 1911), as well as Alexander Meyrick Broadley, *How we Defended Arábi and his Friends: A Story of Egypt and the Egyptians* (1884; new edition Cairo: RAPAC, 1980).

For Guizot, see Larry Siedentop's long and excellent introduction to François Guizot, *The History of Civilization in Europe* (1864; trans. William Hazlitt, London: Penguin Books, 1997), and of course Guizot's own book.

For freemasonry, see A. Albert Kudsi-Zadeh, "Afghani and Freemasonry in Egypt," *Journal of the American Oriental Society* 92 (1972), pp. 25–35, Karim Wissa, "Freemasonry in Egypt 1798–1921: A Study in Cultural and Political Encounters," *Bulletin of the School of Oriental and African Studies* 16, no. 2 (1989), pp. 143–61, and Matthew Scanlan, "Freemasonry Serving Egypt," *Freemasonry Today* 31 (Winter 2005), p. 31.

For the press, see Ami Ayalon, *The Press in the Arab Middle East: A History* (New York: Oxford University Press, 1995), and A. Albert Kudsi-Zadeh, "The Emergence of Political Journalism in Egypt," *The Muslim World* 70 (1980), pp. 47–55.

See also the sources for Muhammad Abduh given in the notes on further reading for Chapter One.

# CHAPTER 3

For Cairo, see Elie Kedourie, *Afghani and 'Abduh: An Essay on Religious Unbelief and Political Activism in Modern Islam* (London: Cass, 1966). See also two sources already suggested in the notes on further reading for Chapter Two: Broadley, *How we Defended Arábi*, and Blunt, *Secret History*.

For *Al-Waqa'i al-misriyya*, see Malcolm H. Kerr, *Islamic Reform: The Political and Legal Theories of Muhammad Abduh and Rashid Rida* (Berkeley: University of California Press, 1966).

For the Damascus Salafis, see Itzchak Weismann, "Between Sufi Reformism and Modernist Rationalism: A Reappraisal of the Origins of the Salafiyya from the Damascene Angle," *Die Welt des Islams* 41 (2001), pp. 206–37.

For Beirut, see Jens Hanssen, *Fin de siècle Beirut: The Making of an Ottoman Provincial Capital* (New York: Oxford University Press, 2005).

## CHAPTER 4

For events in Paris, see the source for Afghani suggested in the notes on further reading for Chapter One, Keddie, *Sayyid Jamal al-Din*. See also Blunt, *Gordon at Khartoum*, already suggested in the notes for Chapter Two.

For the reception of *Al-Urwa al-wuthqa* in India, see Aziz Ahmad, "Afghani's Indian Contacts," *Journal of the American Oriental Society* 89 (1969), p. 482.

## CHAPTER 5

The best source for the basic narrative of these years is Uthman Amin, *Muhammad Abduh*, already suggested in the notes for Chapter One. Also useful are Keddie, *Sayyid Jamal al-Din,* already suggested in the notes for Chapter One, and Hanssen, *Fin de siècle Beirut*, in the notes for Chapter Three.

For the text of *Risalat al-tawhid*, the original edition is Muhammad Abduh, *Risalat al-tawhid* (Cairo: Matba'a al-kubra al-amiriya, 1897). The only English translation is by Ishaq Nusa'ad and Kenneth Cragg, as *The Theology of Unity* (London: George Allen & Unwin, 1966).

Also of interest are (for Taylor) Thomas Prasch, "Which God for Africa: The Islamic–Christian Missionary Debate in Late-Victorian England," *Victorian Studies* 33 (1989), Elie Kedourie, "The Death of Adib Ishaq," *Middle Eastern Studies* 9 (1973), pp. 97–8, and Marwa Elshakry, "The Gospel of Science and American Evangelism in Late Ottoman Beirut," *Past and Present* 196 (2007), pp. 212–23.

## CHAPTER 6

See, again, Uthman Amin, *Muhammad Abduh*, first suggested in the notes on further reading for Chapter One. For the Azhar and the Mufti, see A. Chris Eccel, *Egypt, Islam and Social Change: Al-Azhar in Conflict and Accommodation* (Berlin: Schwarz, 1984), and Jakob Skovgaard-Petersen, *Defining Islam for the Egyptian State: Muftis and Fatwas of the Dar al-Ifta* (Leiden: Brill, 1997).

For the law, see Byron D. Cannon, "Social Tensions and the Teaching of European Law in Egypt Before 1900," *History of Education Quarterly* 15, no. 3 (Autumn 1975), pp. 299–315.

For the khedive, an accessible source is Khedive Abbas Hilmi II, *Memoirs: The Last Khedive of Egypt* (1940; trans. & ed. Amira Sonbol, Reading: Ithaca Press, 1988).

For an unusual and interesting view of "reform," see Timothy Mitchell, *Colonizing Egypt* (Berkeley: University of California Press, 1991).

## CHAPTER 7

See, again, Uthman Amin, *Muhammad Abduh*, suggested in the notes on further reading for Chapter One. See also Ayalon, *The Press in the Arab Middle East*, already suggested in the notes for Chapter Two, and Jamal Mohammed Ahmed, *The Intellectual Origins of Egyptian Nationalism* (London: Oxford University Press, 1960).

For the Azhar lectures as recorded and edited by Rida, see *Tafsir al-Quran al-hakim al-mushtahar bi-ism Tafsir al-Manar*, ed. Muhammad Rashid Rida (Cairo: Dar al-Manar, 1906–1935). For a commentary, see Jacques Jomier, *Le commentaire coranique du Manar: tendances modernes d'exégèse coranique en Egypte* (Paris: G. P. Maisonneuve, 1954).

For Farah Antun, see Donald Malcolm Reid, *The Odyssey of Farah Antun: A Syrian Christian's Quest for Secularism* (Minneapolis: Bibliotheca Islamica, 1975).

## CHAPTER 8

See, again, Uthman Amin, *Muhammad Abduh*, first suggested in the notes for Chapter One. See also Skovgaard-Petersen, *Defining Islam for the Egyptian State*, already suggested in the notes for Chapter Six.

For Islam in South Africa, see Ibrahim Mahomed Mahida, "History of Muslims in South Africa," *South African History Online*, http://www.sahistory.org.za/pages/library-resources/online%20books/history-muslims/1800s.htm.

## CHAPTER 9

The best source for the opposition to Muhammad Abduh is Indira Falk Gesink, "Beyond Modernism: Opposition and Negotiation in the Azhar Reform Movement, 1870–1911," unpublished PhD thesis, Washington University, St. Louis, 2000. It is to be hoped that this thesis will soon be published. Also of use is, once again, Uthman Amin, *Muhammad Abduh*, first suggested in the notes for Chapter One.

Taha Husayn's *Al-ayyam* is available in translation as *The Days: Taha Husayn, his Autobiography in Three Parts*, ed. E. H. Paxton, Hilary Wayment and Kenneth Cragg (Cairo: AUC Press, 1997).

For Muhammad Abduh in Algeria, see Rachid Bencheneb, "Le séjour du Šayh 'Abduh en Algérie (1903)," *Studia Islamica* 53 (1981), pp. 121–35.

## CHAPTER 10

For politics, Walid Kazziha, "The Jaridah-Ummah Group and Egyptian Politics," *Middle Eastern Studies* 13 (1977), pp. 373–85.

For the reception of Abduh, Mohamed Haddad, "Les oeuvres de 'Abduh: histoire d'une manipulation," *Institut de Belles Lettres Arabes* (Tunis) 60 (1997), pp. 197–222 and Mohamed Haddad, "Abduh et ses lecteurs: pour une histoire critique des lectures de M. 'Abduh," *Arabica* 45 (1998), pp. 22–49.

For insurance, Samir Mankabady, "Insurance and Islamic Law: The Islamic Insurance Company," *Arab Law Quarterly* 4, no. 3 (August 1989), pp. 200–201.

# BIBLIOGRAPHY

Abbas Hilmi II, Khedive. *Memoirs: The Last Khedive of Egypt* (1940), trans. and ed. Amira Sonbol. Reading: Ithaca Press, 1988.
Abduh, Muhammad: see Muhammad Abduh
Adams, Charles C. *Islam and Modernism in Egypt: A Study of the Modern Reform Movement Inaugurated by Muhammad 'Abduh*. London: Oxford University Press, 1933.
Afghani, Jamal al-Din. *Haqiqat-i mazhab-i naichun*. Hyderabad, 1881.
―― Letter to the editor. *Journal des débats politiques et littéraires*, May 18, 1883, p. 3.
Ahmad, Aziz: see Aziz Ahmad.
Ahmed, Jamal Mohammed: see Jamal Mohammed Ahmed.
Amin, Uthman: see Uthman Amin.
"Anglais en Egypte," les. *Journal des débats*, April 6, 1883, p. 2.
Ayalon, Ami. *The Press in the Arab Middle East: A History*. New York: Oxford University Press, 1995.
Aziz Ahmad. "Afghani's Indian Contacts." *Journal of the American Oriental Society* 89 (1969), pp. 476–504.
Beinin, Joel. "Islamic Responses to the Capitalist Penetration of the Middle East." In *The Islamic Impulse*, ed. Barbara F. Stowasser. Washington: Croom Helm, 1987, pp. 87–106.
Bencheneb, Rachid. "Le séjour du šayh 'Abduh en Algérie (1903)." *Studia Islamica* 53 (1981), pp. 121–35.
Blunt, Wilfrid Scawen. *Secret History of the English Occupation of Egypt: Being a Personal Narrative of Events* (1907). New York: H. Fertig, 1967.
―― *Gordon at Khartoum: Being a Personal Narrative of Events in Continuation of a Secret History of the English Occupation of Egypt*. London: Swift, 1911.
Broadley, Alexander Meyrick. *How we Defended Arábi and his Friends: A Story of Egypt and the Egyptians* (1884). Cairo: RAPAC, 1980.
Cannon, Byron D. "Social Tensions and the Teaching of European Law in Egypt Before 1900." *History of Education Quarterly* 15, no. 3 (Autumn 1975), pp. 299–315.

Cole, Juan R. I. "Muhammad 'Abduh and Rashid Rida: A Dialogue on the Baha'i Faith." *World Order* 15, nos. 3–4 (Spring/Summer 1981), pp. 7–16.

—— *Colonialism and Revolution in the Middle East: Social and Cultural Origins of Egypt's 'Urabi Movement*. Princeton: Princeton University Press, 1993.

Cromer, Earl of. *Modern Egypt*. London: Macmillan, 1908.

—— *Abbas II*. London: Macmillan, 1915.

De Jong, Fred. "Madaniyya." *Encyclopaedia of Islam*, 2nd edition.

Eccel, A. Chris. *Egypt, Islam and Social Change: Al-Azhar in Conflict and Accommodation*. Berlin: Schwarz, 1984.

Eickelman, Dale F. "The Art of Memory: Islamic Education and its Social Reproduction." *Comparative Studies in Society and History* 20 (1978), pp. 485–516.

Elshakry, Marwa. "The Gospel of Science and American Evangelism in Late Ottoman Beirut." *Past and Present* 196 (2007), pp. 212–23.

Falk Gesink, Indira. "Beyond Modernism: Opposition and Negotiation in the Azhar Reform Movement, 1870–1911." Unpublished PhD thesis, Washington University, St. Louis, 2000.

Goldschmidt, Arthur. *Biographical Dictionary of Modern Egypt*. Boulder: Lynne Rienner, 2000.

Gottheil, Richard. "Mohammed Abduh, Late Mufti of Egypt." *Journal of the American Oriental Society* 28 (1907), p. 196.

Guizot, François. *The History of Civilization in Europe* (1864). Trans. William Hazlitt. London: Penguin Books, 1997.

Haddad, Mohamed. "Les oeuvres de 'Abduh: histoire d'une manipulation." *Institut de Belles Lettres Arabes* (Tunis) 60 (1997), pp. 197–222.

—— "Abduh et ses lecteurs: pour une histoire critique des lectures de M. 'Abduh." *Arabica* 45 (1998), pp. 22–49.

Hanssen, Jens. *Fin de siècle Beirut: The Making of an Ottoman Provincial Capital*. New York: Oxford University Press, 2005.

Herrera, Linda. "Overlapping Modernities: From Christian Missionary to Muslim Reform Schooling in Egypt." CIAO Working Paper, 2001.

Hildenbrandt, Thomas. "Waren Ğamal ad-Din al-Afġani und Muhammad 'Abduh Neo-Mu'taziliten?" *Die Welt des Islams* 42 (2002), pp. 205–62.

Hunter, F. Robert. *Egypt under the Khedives, 1805–1879: From Household Government to Modern Bureaucracy*. Pittsburgh: University of Pittsburgh Press, 1984.

Husayn, Taha: see Taha Husayn.
Ibrahim Mahomed Mahida. "History of Muslims in South Africa." *South African History Online*, http://www.sahistory.org.za/pages/library-resources/online%20books/history-muslims/1800s.htm.
Jamal Mohammed Ahmed. *The Intellectual Origins of Egyptian Nationalism*. London: Oxford University Press, 1960.
Jomier, Jacques. *Le commentaire coranique du Manar: tendances modernes d'exégèse coranique en Egypte*. Paris: G. P. Maisonneuve, 1954.
Kazziha, Walid. "The Jaridah-Ummah Group and Egyptian Politics." *Middle Eastern Studies* 13 (1977), pp. 373–85.
Keddie, Nikki. *An Islamic Response to Imperialism: Political and Religious Writings of Sayyid Jamal ad-Din "al-Afghani" including a translation of the Refutation of the Materialists from the original Persian by Nikki R. Keddie and Hamid Algar*. Berkeley: University of California Press, 1968.
—— *Sayyid Jamal al-Din "al-Afghani": A Political Biography*. Berkeley: University of California Press, 1972.
Kedourie, Elie. *Afghani and 'Abduh: An Essay on Religious Unbelief and Political Activism in Modern Islam*. London: Cass, 1966.
—— "The death of Adib Ishaq." *Middle Eastern Studies* 9 (1973), pp. 31–6.
Kerr, Malcolm H. *Islamic Reform: The Political and Legal Theories of Muhammad Abduh and Rashid Rida*. Berkeley: University of California Press, 1966.
Klemke, Andreas. *Stiftungen im muslimischen Rechtsleben des neuzeitlichen Ägypten*. Frankfurt: Heidelberger Orientalistischer Studien, 1991.
Köhler, Werner, and Simon P. Hardy. "Zentralblatt für Bakteriologie – 100 years ago: Early considerations of the El Tor vibrios." *International Journal of Medical Microbiology* 296 (2006), pp. 333–40.
Kudsi-Zadeh, A. Albert. "Afghani and Freemasonry in Egypt." *Journal of the American Oriental Society* 92 (1972), pp. 25–35.
—— "The Emergence of Political Journalism in Egypt." *The Muslim World* 70 (1980), pp. 47–55.
Mahida, Ibrahim Mahomed: see Ibrahim Mahomed Mahida.
Mankabady, Samir. "Insurance and Islamic Law: The Islamic Insurance Company." *Arab Law Quarterly* 4, no. 3 (August 1989), pp. 199–205.
Marsot, Afaf Lutfi Al-Sayyid. "The Cartoon in Egypt." *Comparative Studies in Society and History* 13, no. 1 (January 1971), pp. 2–15.
Mayeur-Jaouen, Catherine. "Tanta." *Encyclopaedia of Islam*, 2nd edition.

Michel, B., and Moustapha Abdel Razik. "Introduction sur la vie et les idées du Cheikh Mohammed Abdou." Introduction to *Rissalat al Tawhid: exposé de la religion musulmane*. Paris: P. Geuthner, 1925.

Mitchell, Timothy. *Colonizing Egypt*. Berkeley: University of California Press, 1991.

Muhammad Abduh. *Risalat al-waridat fi sirr al-tajalliyyat*. Manuscript, 1874.

—— *Al-taliqat ala sharh al-Dawani li'l-aqaid al-Adudiyya*. Manuscript, 1876.

—— *Risalat al-tawhid*. Cairo: Matba'a al-kubra al-amiriyya, 1897.

—— *Tafsir al-fatiha*. Cairo, 1901.

—— *Tafsir al-Quran al-hakim al-mushtahar bi-ism Tafsir al-Manar*, ed. Muhammad Rashid Rida. Cairo: Dar al-Manar, 1906–35.

—— *Al-amal al-kamila li'l-imam Muhammad Abduh*, ed. Muhammad Imara. Beirut: Al-mu'assasa al-Arabiya li'l-dirasat wa al-nashr, 1972–74, 6 vols.

Ostle, Robin. "Modern Egyptian Renaissance Man." *Bulletin of the School of Oriental and African Studies* 57 (1994), pp. 184–92.

Prasch, Thomas. "Which God for Africa: The Islamic–Christian Missionary Debate in Late-Victorian England." *Victorian Studies* 33 (1989), pp. 51–73.

Reid, Donald Malcolm. *The Odyssey of Farah Antun: A Syrian Christian's Quest for Secularism*. Minneapolis: Bibliotheca Islamica, 1975.

Renan, Ernest. "L'islamisme et la science." *Journal des débats politiques et littéraires*, March 30, 1883, pp. 2–3.

—— Letter to the editor. *Journal des débats politiques et littéraires*, May 19, 1883, p. 3.

Rida, Muhammad Rashid. *Tarikh al-ustadh al-imam al-shaykh Muhammad Abduh*. Cairo: Matba'at al-manar, 1906.

Rizk, Yunan Labib. "Demise of the Red Headgear." *Al-Ahram Weekly* 525 (March 15, 2001).

Roff, William R. "Kaum Muda – Kaum Tua: Innovation and Reaction amongst the Malays, 1900–1941." In *Papers on Malayan History*, ed. K. G. Tregonning. Singapore: Journal of South-East Asian History, 1962, pp. 162–92.

Salomon, Noah. "Undoing the Mahdiyya: British Colonialism as Religious Reform in the Anglo-Egyptian Sudan, 1898–1914." University of

Chicago Divinity School working paper, May 2004. Available http://marty-center.uchicago.edu/webforum/052004/salomon.pdf.

Scanlan, Matthew. "Freemasonry Serving Egypt." *Freemasonry Today* 31 (Winter 2005), p. 31.

Scharbrodt, Oliver. "The Salafiyya and Sufism: Muhammad 'Abduh and his *Risalat al-waridat* (Treatise on mystical inspirations)." *Bulletin of the School of Oriental and African Studies* 70 (2007), pp. 89–115.

Siedentop, Larry. "Introduction." In *The History of Civilization in Europe* (1864) by François Guizot. London: Penguin Books, 1997.

Skovgaard-Petersen, Jakob. *Defining Islam for the Egyptian State: Muftis and Fatwas of the Dar al-Ifta*. Leiden: Brill, 1997.

Smallman-Raynor, Matthew, and Andrew D. Cliff, "The Philippines Insurrection and the 1902–4 Cholera Epidemic." *Journal of Historical Geography* 24, no. 1 (January 1998), pp. 69–89.

Taha Husayn. *Al-ayyam*. Trans. as *The Days: Taha Husayn, his Autobiography in Three Parts*, ed. E. H. Paxton, Hilary Wayment, and Kenneth Cragg. Cairo: AUC Press, 1997.

Taylor, Isaac. *Leaves from an Egyptian Notebook*. London: Kegan Paul, Trench, 1888.

Uthman Amin. *Muhammad Abduh*. Cairo: Dar ihya al-kutub al-arabiyya, 1944. Trans. Charles Wendell. Washington, DC: American Council of Learned Societies, 1953.

Van Ess, Josef. "Libanesische Mizellen: 6. Die Yashrutiya." *Die Welt des Islams* 16 (1975), pp. 1–103.

Weismann, Itzchak. "Between Sufi Reformism and Modernist Rationalism: A Reappraisal of the Origins of the Salafiyya from the Damascene Angle." *Die Welt des Islams* 41 (2001), pp. 206–37.

Wissa, Karim. "Freemasonry in Egypt 1798–1921: A Study in Cultural and Political Encounters." *Bulletin of the School of Oriental and African Studies* 16, no. 2 (1989), pp. 143–61.

# INDEX

*For Arabs and Ottomans, see under first name*

Abbas Hilmi, Khedive 72, 74–5, 77–8, 81, 115, 116
   clashes with Muhammad Abduh 97, 107–13
Abd al-Halim, Prince 20, 27, 42
Abd al-Hamid, Sultan 49–50, 53, 62, 88
Abd al-Qadir, Amir 35, 58
Abd al-Rahman Kuraha 117–18
Abd al-Salam al-Muwaylihi 25
Abduh ibn Hasan Khayrallah 1–2, 4
Abdullah al-Nadim 10, 22, 32
Abdullahi Ahmed An-Na'im 121
Abu Ali al-Husayn ibn Abdullah ibn Sina 11, 38
Abu Bakr Muhammad Ibn al-Arabi al-Maliki 99, 100, 111
*Abu naddara* 21–2, 105
Abu Tammam Habib ibn Aws al-Ta'i 60
Abu Turab 36, 39
Abu Zayd Abd al-Rahman ibn Khaldun 11, 17, 60
Abu'l-Walid Muhammad ibn Rushd 89
Adib Ishaq 10, 22–4, 44, 63
Afghani, *see* Jamal al-Din al-Afghani
Afghanistan 8, 18
agnosticism 113–14
   *see also* atheism; freedom of thought; religiosity
*ahliyya* degree 75–6
Ahmad al-Badawi 2, 111
Ahmad ibn Miskawayh 16
Ahmad Khan 30, 39–40, 58, 60, 66
Ahmad Lutfi 92, 116, 117
Ahmad Pasha al-Minshawi 91–2
Ahmad Shafiq Pasha 113
Ahmad Urabi, Colonel 31–5, 107
*Ahram, Al-* 22, 105, 111, 125
Alexandria 5, 29, 34, 36, 44, 113, 124

Algeria 101–2
Ali ibn Abi Talib, Imam 60
Ali Mubarak 7
Ali Yusuf 87, 101
Aligarh 40
*alimiyya* degree 7, 13, 76
appointments of Muhammad Abduh 72–4, 77–8, 83
Arabic language
   Afghani's 10
   colloquial 22, 105
   improvement of 30
   little known in India 45
   Muhammad Abduh's 15, 33, 60
   religious duty to preserve 54
   Semitic 52
   use of by educated 90
   use of by elite 20, 24, 29, 120
Arabic literature 60, 76, 92, 124
Aristotle 11, 16
Aryan, *see* race
assassination 23, 26, 58
atheism 38, 63–4
   *see also* agnosticism; infidelity; religiosity
autocracy 26, 31–2, 50, 88
   *see also* liberty; tyranny
Avicenna 11, 38
Azhar
   administration of 7, 74–5; *see also* Azhar Administrative Council
   conditions at 6–7
   hostile to Afghani 27
   hostile to Muhammad Abduh 12–13, 103–4, 106–7, 109
   lectures of Muhammad Abduh at 84–7
   Muhammad Abduh studies at 7–8, 12–13

Azhar (cont.):
  Muhammad Abduh teaches at 13, 15–16, 83–7
  publications of 91
  rector of 7, 13, 75, 78, 106–7, 109
  reform of 7, 74–6, 77
Azhar Administrative Council 75–6, 79, 84, 101, 111–12
Azhar Council 7

backwardness, see decline
Badi al-Zaman al-Hamadhani 60
Baha'ism 23, 62
Bakunin, Mikhail 19
Baring, Sir Evelyn, see Cromer, Lord
Beirut 36, 39, 42, 45, 59–63, 64, 71–2, 88
*bida* 30, 123
birth of Muhammad Abduh 1
Blunt, Wilfrid 33, 45–8, 50, 51, 55, 57–8, 62, 93
Borg, Raphael 19
Brighton 92–3
Britain, see Ahmad Urabi; Brighton; Cromer; London; Wafd Party
Broadley, Alexander 21, 33, 34
Butrus Ghali Pasha 21, 114

Cairo University, see Egyptian University
Charles Stone Pasha, General 24
childhood
  of Muhammad Abduh 1–5
  views of Spencer on 93
children of Muhammad Abduh 42, 59–60
cholera 109–10
Christianity 19–20, 38, 40, 48–9, 106, 111
  see also inter-religious relations; missionaries; Protestantism
Christians, Orthodox and oriental 2, 23–4, 35, 36, 49, 55, 60, 63, 84, 102
Churchill, Lord Randolph 47
civilization, see European civilization; progress
clothing, see fez; hat; shoes
Commission of Inquiry 18, 71
Commission of the Public Debt 18
Commission on Azhar reform 74–5

Commission on education of Sharia Court judges 112, 115
Commission on interest 87, 110
Commission on Ottoman educational reform 61
community, see identity; nationalism; Ottoman community
constitutional government 16, 25–6, 31–3, 48–50
  see also liberty
Council, see Azhar Administrative Council; Azhar Council; Council for Endowments; Treasury Council
Council for Endowments 83, 95–6, 105, 110
Court of Appeal
  national 74, 77
  Sharia 78, 118
court system 72–3, 79–80
courts, see mixed courts; national courts; Sharia Courts
Cragg, Kenneth 125
Cromer, Lord 71–2, 78, 108
  and Muhammad Abduh 72, 102, 109, 110, 112, 113–14
  after Muhammad Abduh's death 115–16
crusades 17, 58, 67

Damascus 35
Dar al-Ulum 15, 17, 72, 76
Darwin 39–40, 64, 87
  see also evolution
Darwish, uncle 4–5, 8, 13
*dawsa* 30
death of Muhammad Abduh 113
decay, see decline
decline 38, 67, 87, 105, 123; see also philosophy, alleged Arab hostility to
development, see progress
disease 68, 109
  see also hygiene
dress, see fez; hat; shoes
Dumas, Alexandre 74

education
  primary 30, 75–6, 92–3, 106, 112; see also school in Tanta

secondary 30, 60–1, 112
  higher 91–2; see also Azhar; Egyptian University; school for Sharia Court judges
Egyptian Press Association 105
Egyptian University 91–1, 115, 116, 123, 124
England, see Ahmad Urabi; Brighton; Cromer; London; Wafd Party
Enlightenment 16, 64
equity, see maslaha
European civilization 16–18, 58, 67, 77, 101, 122
European holidays 76–7
evolution 69
  see also Darwin
exegesis, see methodology; tafsir

Fahmi, Leon 108
*Falsafat al-ijtima* 17
family of Muhammad Abduh 42, 59–60
Farah Antun 88–9
Farsi 39
fatalism 67, 70
  see also predestination
fatwa 83, 84, 95–7, 97–9, 101
fez 15, 46, 98, 118
finance
  consumer 95–6, 117–18
  Islamic 118
finances
  of Egyptian government 18, 25, 71
  of émigrés 43
  of ulema 6, 83
foreign languages 74
free will, see predestination
freedom of thought 23, 38–9, 74, 124, 126
  see also liberty
Freemasonry 22, 35, 44
  and Egyptian politics 20–6; see also Kawkab al-Sharq
  and Muhammad Abduh in later years 114, 123
  nature of 19–20, 21, 24
French language 36, 43, 61, 64, 74, 92
Fuad I University, see Egyptian University

Garibaldi, Giuseppe 19

Geneva 77
God 40, 52–3, 113; see also revelation
  existence of 11, 65
  as the origin of truth 23
  as a prior or first cause 65, 68, 89
  role of 67–8, 89
Gorst, Sir Eldon 116
government, see autocracy; constitutional government; liberty; revolution; tyranny
Grand Orient 20, 24, 25, 114
Great Britain, see Ahmad Urabi; Brighton; Cromer; London; Wafd Party
Greece
  ancient 16, 37
  modern 2, 108, 124
Guerville, Amédée de 91
Guizot, François 16–17, 58, 60, 67, 68, 86, 123

hadith 3, 55, 66, 68, 86, 99–100, 119–20, 123
hajj pilgrimage 106, 109–10
Hanotaux, Gabriel 87
*Haqiqat-i mazhab-i naichun* 39, 51–2, 65–6
Hasan al-Banna 119
Hassuna al-Nawawi 77–8
hat 98
  see also fez; identity
*Himarat Munyati* 105–7, 110
history, see Ibn Khaldun; Guizot; *Risalat al-tawhid*
Howard, George, Earl of Carlisle 47
Husayn al-Jisr 64, 88
hygiene 7, 76
  see also disease

Ibn Khaldun 11, 17, 60
Ibn Rushd 89
Ibn Sina 11, 38
Ibn Taymiyya 122–3
Ibrahim al-Bajuri 7
Ibrahim al-Laqqani 22, 36, 43
Ibrahim al-Muwaylihi 43, 45, 59
identity
  of Muhammad Abduh 15, 46–7, 60
  national 101–2, 127
images 101

India 30, 39–40, 45, 46, 49, 50, 66, 71, 98
  see also Ahmad Khan; Jamal al-Din al-Afghani
infidelity 38, 113–14
  see also agnosticism; atheism; religiosity
insurance 96–7, 100, 117–18
intercession 67
interpretation of Muhammad Abduh
  general 121–6
  impact on Egypt 115–17
  impact on Islam 117–21
inter-religious relations 55, 61–3, 69–70, 88–9, 98–9
interest, financial 67, 95–7, 105, 110
Iran, see Persia
Islam 64, 104, 127
  see also prayer; religiosity; revelation; Sharia
Islamic finance 118
  see also finance, consumer
Ismail, Khedive
  reforms 7, 10, 15
  opposition to 18, 20–2, 24–6, 103
  in exile 45
Istanbul 9–10, 45, 58, 61, 87, 101, 108
Italy 19, 21, 37, 45, 61

Jamal al-Din al-Afghani
  early career 9–10
  in Cairo 8–9, 10–12
  foments revolution in Egypt 18–27
  expelled from Egypt 27
  in Paris 36–7, 44–5, 49–52
  Muhammad Abduh leaves 57
  later career 57–8
  death 58
  religiosity of 38–41
  later views of 124–6
Jarida, Al- 116
Jews 10, 23, 49–50, 55, 62, 69, 85, 99, 102
jihad 23–4, 54–5
Journal des débats 36–8
journalism; see also opposition to Muhammad Abduh; press
  British 25–6, 51
  Egyptian 10, 21–4, 29

French 36–8
Islamic 90–1; see also Urwa al-wuthqa
Muhammad Abduh's 29–31; see also Urwa al-wuthqa
Ottoman and Syrian 43, 88
popular 21–2, 105–7
Judaism, see Jews
jurisprudence, see methodology; usul al-fiqh

Kant, Immanuel 74
Kawkab al-Sharq 19–21, 24–5, 26
Kedourie, Elie 125–6
Kerr, Malcolm 125
Khedival Law School 73
Khedival School of Languages 15
khedive 10
  see also Abbas Hilmi; Ismail; Tawfiq

Labouchere, Henry 47–8
languages, see Arabic; Farsi; French
Latif Salim, Major 25
law; see also court system
  of God, see Sharia
  reform 79–81
  rule of 73–4; see also liberty
Law School, Khedival 73
Legislative Council 83
Leon Fahmi 108
liberty 17, 21, 23, 27, 32, 34–5, 51, 65–6
  see also freedom of thought; law, rule of
Liwa, Al- 100
lodge, see Freemasonry; Kawkab al-Sharq
London 47–9, 50, 57–8
  see also United Grand Lodge

McIlwraith, Malcolm 77–8, 80
Madaniyya 4–5, 35
madhhabs 80–1, 84, 98, 111
  demise of 118–20, 123; see also talfiq; taqlid
Mahallat Nasr 2, 3–4, 27, 29
Mahdi 45–6
Mahmud Sami Pasha al-Barudi 33
Malaya 90
Manar, Al- 84–5, 88–90, 95, 111, 114, 121, 128

marriage; *see also* polygamy
  of Muhammad Abduh 42, 59–60
Marx, Karl 17
*maslaha* 80, 119
Masonry, *see* Freemasonry; Kawkab al-Sharq
meat 98–9, 110–11, 118
Mecca 106, 109, 119; *see also* hajj pilgrimage
  in history 54, 67, 86, 87
Medina 4, 119
Mehmet Ali Pasha 1, 6, 10, 18, 20, 108
methodology 55, 66, 99–100, 120–1, 127
Mill, John Stuart 17
*Mirat al-sharq* 22
Mirza Muhammad Baqir 48–9, 62
*Misr* (newspaper) 22
*Misr al-fatat* 22
missionaries, Christian 30, 61, 92
mixed courts 71, 95
modernism 60, 96, 101–2, 121, 127–8
  *see also* Ahmad Khan
modernity 70
  of Muhammad Abduh 33, 64, 68, 70, 92
modernization
  of Egypt 9, 15, 26, 117; *see also* Azhar reform; education; law reform
  of Ottoman Empire 50
Mohamed Haddad 126
Mohammed Arkoun 121
*Mu'ayyad, Al-* 87, 105
Mufti
  duties of 77–8, 83–4
  Muhammad Abduh as 81, 83–4; *see also* fatwa
Muhammad, Prophet 54, 65, 67, 69
  *see also* bida; hadith; revelation
Muhammad Abd al-Halim, Prince 20, 27, 42
Muhammad al-Farabi 11
Muhammad al-Madani 4–5
Muhammad al-Sharbatli 105
Muhammad Arkoun 121
Muhammad Bakhit 117
Muhammad Baqir, Mirza 48–9, 62
Muhammad Bey Rasim 113

Muhammad Haddad 126
Muhammad ibn Abd al-Wahhab 119–20, 126
Muhammad Sharif Pasha 20, 25–7, 31, 36, 44
Muhammad Talaat Harb 92, 116–17
Muhyi al-Din Bey Humada 36, 60
Muhyi al-Din ibn al-Arabi 35
Mulla Sadra 11
*Muqattam, Al-* 105, 111
Muslim Benevolent Society 92–3
Mustafa Abd al-Raziq 123–4
Mustafa Fahmi 91
Mustafa Kamil 110
Mustafa Riyad Pasha 10, 15, 18–19, 22, 25, 27, 29, 31, 36
Mutazila 12–13
mysticism 11–12, 21, 35
  *see also* Sufism

Nasr Abu Zayd 121
national courts 73, 74, 77, 79–80
nationalism; *see also* identity
  early 21, 23–4, 46, 47, 49–51; *see also* Ahmad Urabi
  khedival 75
  later 109, 116–17, 122, 124, 127–8
native courts, *see* national courts
nature, laws of 39–41
  *see also* science
Nazli Fadil, Princess 91
Neo-Sufism 4–5, 35
newspaper, *see by title*
  *see also* journalism
Nihilism 23, 27
Nubar Pasha 25

Omar Lutfi 92, 116
opposition to Muhammad Abduh
  Azhar 103–4, 106–7, 109
  khedive 97, 107–13
  press 105–7, 110–11
Orientalism 36, 66
Osama bin Laden 54, 126
Ottoman community 24, 88
Ottoman Empire
  Afghani and 9, 18, 45, 49–51, 57–8
  Egypt and 1, 26, 71, 77–8

Ottoman Empire (*cont.*):
  exiles from 43
  government of 21, 43, 108
  modernization of 9
  Muhammad Abduh in 35–6, 59–91, 101
  Muhammad Abduh on 51
Ottoman Islam 10, 80, 97–8, 103
Ottoman Turkish language 24, 29

Paris 42–55, 91, 99
  *see also* Grand Orient
Parnell, Charles Stewart 47
pasha 9
  *see also individuals by name*
patriotism, *see* nationalism
Persia 12, 18, 23, 37, 51, 62
  *see also* Jamal al-Din al-Afghani; Shi'ism
Persian language 39
philosophy; *see also* reason
  alleged Arab hostility to 37–9, 41, 89
  of history, *see* Guizot; Ibn Khaldun
  Islamic 11–12, 65; *see also* mysticism
  Western 64, 74, 124
photography 47, 106–7
Plotinus 11
politics, *see* autocracy; constitutional government; liberty; revolution; theocracy; tyranny
polygamy 2, 30, 39, 86, 100
prayer 8–9, 54, 98
  intercessory 67
  wearing shoes 101, 114
predestination 13, 65, 67–8, 86, 87–8, 105–6
press, *see* journalism
progress 9, 31, 33, 37, 51, 69–70, 75–6, 84, 88–9, 95, 118
prophecy 9–10, 11, 63, 69
  *see also* revelation
Protestantism 61–7
  *see also* Reformation

Quran 40; *see also* methodology; revelation; *tafsir*; *usul al-fiqh*
  createdness of 48–9
  learned by Muhammad Abduh 2
  logic of 65
  use of by Afghani and in *Al-Urwa al-wuthqa* 44, 52–5
  use of in Azhar lectures 85–7

race 37, 51–2, 87–8
*Radd ala al-dahriyyin, Al-*, see *Haqiqat-i mazhab-i naichun*
Rashid Rida 88–9, 114, 119, 121–4, 125
reason; *see also* Enlightenment; philosophy
  Afghani on 39, 41
  Ibn Abd al-Wahhab on 119
  Muhammad Abduh on 54–4, 65–9, 87, 119
  opposed to revelation 13
  theocracy as enemy of 16–17, 66
rector, *see* Azhar, rector of
Reformation 16, 64, 67, 91
religiosity; *see also* agnosticism; atheism; freedom of thought; infidelity
  of Jamal al-Din al-Afghani 38–41
  of Muhammad Abduh 36, 38–41, 61–3, 113–14
renaissance, Egyptian 22, 117, 124
Renan, Ernest 36–9
representative government, *see* constitutional government; liberty
resignation of Muhammad Abduh 111–12
revelation; *see also* prophecy; Quran
  Afghani on 9–10
  Azhari views on 13, 99–100
  Muhammad Abduh on 11, 13, 48–9, 65, 67, 69, 99
revolution 17, 19, 21, 23, 116, 127
Rifaa Bey 29
*Risalat al-tawhid* 63–70
*Risalat al-waridat* 11–12
Russia 58, 90
  *see also* Nihilism

Saad al-Din al-Taftazani 13
Saad al-Din Humada 60
Saad Zaghlul
  as a young man 10–11, 20, 30, 46
  in middle age 91–2, 114, 122
  later career of 50, 115–16, 123
Sadra, Mulla 11
Safiya Fahmi 91
Salafism 35, 66–7, 126

*salat, see* prayer
Salim al-Naqqash 22, 24
Salim Anhuri 22
Scandinavia 19
scholars
  Islamic, *see* ulema
  Western, *see* philosophy; science
scholarship, *see* education
school for Sharia Court judges 79–80, 115, 123
school in Tanta 2–5
School of Languages, Khedival 15
Schopenhauer, Arthur 74
science 37, 86–7, 91; *see also* Darwin; evolution; nature; progress; reason
  teaching of 60, 64, 92
Semitic, *see* Arabic language; race
Sharia 38, 52–3, 64, 80, 88–9, 95, 96–7, 99, 118; *see also* revelation
  codification 79–80
  Courts 72–3, 75, 77–8, 79–80, 112, 115; *see also* Court of Appeal, Sharia
  judges 79, 112; *see also* school for Sharia Court judges
Shi'ism 8–9, 41
  possible influence on Muhammad Abduh 11–13, 49, 60, 68
shoes, worn while praying 101, 114
slavery 46–7
social utility of religion 39–40, 65
Society for the Revival of Arabic Books 92
South Africa 97–9
Spencer, Herbert 92–3
spy, British 108
Stone Pasha, General Charles 24
Sudan 45–6, 112, 121
Sufism 2, 4, 35, 45; *see also* mysticism; Neo-Sufism
  criticism of by Muhammad Abduh 30, 86, 87–8, 100, 111
  criticism of by Rashid Rida 123
  possible influence on Muhammad Abduh 12–13
  practiced by Muhammad Abduh 5, 7–8; *see also* Madaniyya
Sulayman Abaza Pasha 20
Sultaniyya 60–1, 64

supporters of Muhammad Abduh 105–6, 109, 111, 112, 120–1

*tafsir* 3, 55, 68, 85–6, 88, 96, 100
  *see also* Azhar lectures; *Tafsir al-Manar*
*Tafsir al-Manar* 85, 121, 123
Taha Husayn 104, 124
Taksin Pasha 9–10
Talaat Harb, *see* Muhammad Talaat Harb
*talfiq* 80–1, 90, 119
*Taliqat ala sharh al-Dawani, Al-* 12
Tanta 2–5, 29
Taqi al-Din Ahmad ibn Taymiyya 122–3
*taqlid* 4, 13, 35, 66, 81, 85, 100, 118–20, 123
Tawfiq, Khedive 20, 25–7, 31, 34, 72, 74
Taylor, Isaac 61–3
terrorism 23, 26, 58
Thasos 108
theocracy 16–17
theological disputes 66, 100
Theosophy 46, 62
*Tijara, Al-* 22, 23, 27, 102
Tocqueville, Alexis de 17
Transvaal fatwa 97–9
Treasury Council 83
Tunis 57
Turk, *see* Ottoman
tyranny 34, 50, 51, 66
  *see also* autocracy; liberty

ulema 5, 66, 90–1, 99, 119–20; *see also* Azhar; Ottoman Islam; Sharia Courts; Tanta
  attacked by Muhammad Abduh 54, 64, 103; *see also* freedom of thought; *taqlid*
Umar al-Nasafi 13
Umma Party 116
United Grand Lodge of England 20, 24
Urabi Revolt, *see* Ahmad Urabi
*Urwa al-wuthqa, Al-* (group) 44, 57
*Urwa al-wuthqa, Al-* (newspaper) 44–5, 49–55, 88
*usul al-fiqh* 3, 54–5, 66, 68
  *see also* methodology
usury, *see* interest
Uthman Amin 75, 124

utilitarianism 23, 35, 93, 96–7
  *see also* utility of religion
utility of religion 39–40, 65

Victoria, Queen 62–3
violence 67, 93
  *see also* jihad

Wafd Party 116

Wahhabism 119–20, 126
*Waqa'i al-misriyya, Al-* 29–31, 32, 86
*Watan, Al-* 105, 111
wives of Muhammad Abduh 42, 59–60

Yaqub Sannua 21, 43

*Zahir, Al-* 105, 110, 111